OPPORTUNITIES in

Law Enforcement and Criminal Justice Careers

REVISED EDITION

JAMES STINCHCOMB

VGM Career Books

Chicago   New York   San Francisco   Lisbon   London   Madrid   Mexico City
Milan   New Delhi   San Juan   Seoul   Singapore   Sydney   Toronto

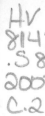

HV
8143
.S86
2003
C.2

The *McGraw-Hill* Companies

Library of Congress Cataloging-in-Publication Data

Stinchcomb, James D.
    Opportunities in law enforcement and criminal justice careers / James
Stinchcomb.—Rev. ed.
        p. cm.—(VGM opportunities series)
    Includes bibliographical references.
    ISBN 0-07-139038-3 (paperback)
    1. Police—Vocational guidance—United States.   2. Law enforcement
—Vocational guidance—United States.   3. Criminal justice,
Administration of—Vocational guidance—United States.   I. Title.   II. Series.

    HV8143 .S86   2003
    363.2'023'73—dc21   2002016839

2 3 4 5 6 7 8 9 0   LBM/LBM   1 0 9 8 7 6 5 4

ISBN 0-07-139038-3

McGraw-Hill books are available at special quantity discounts to use as premiums and
sales promotions, or for use in corporate training programs. For more information,
please write to the Director of Special Sales, Professional Publishing, McGraw-Hill, Two
Penn Plaza, New York, NY 10121-2298. Or contact your local bookstore.

This book is printed on acid-free paper.

CONTENTS

FOREWORD

BEING A CRIMINAL justice practitioner in my former life and a criminal justice professor for a number of years, I am firmly convinced that higher education can produce a cadre of the best and the brightest candidates for criminal justice agencies. For most of us, our ultimate career choice is different from the aspirations we developed as young adults. One of the more valuable aspects of higher education for students is the opportunity to get a sample of possible career choices. The exposure students get by taking courses in various disciplines such as engineering, chemistry, business, sociology, or psychology can provide a glimpse of the nature of various career opportunities. With this preliminary view of career choices, students begin to get a sense of careers in which they can excel.

Also, students who major in criminal justice will discover that career opportunities can be found in law enforcement, corrections, and juvenile justice, as well as within organizations at the local, state, and federal levels of government. For example, there are thousands of law enforcement careers within federal agencies such as the United States Department of Agriculture, the Internal Revenue Service, the Federal Bureau of Investigation, and the Bureau of Alcohol, Tobacco, and Firearms. Moreover, criminal justice students can take advantage of opportunities in the multitude of private security firms that have been expanding at a rapid rate in the last thirty years and that are always in the market for good candidates. Finally, there are a number of criminal justice careers available within military service. Each branch of the service has a military police unit that provides law enforcement duties on military bases. Also, there are elite agencies in the military that perform sensitive and often international investigation work. Regardless of the particular military assignment, civilian criminal justice agencies often prefer to hire individuals with military experience.

Career development really begins after getting your first position in a criminal justice or private security agency. There are a number of specialized roles in almost all organizations that one can aspire to after a few years at the entry level. For example, one may work in narcotics enforcement, fraud, or homicide investigation, or in a number of other law enforcement assignments. In addition, opportunities for promotion to supervisory positions will eventually become available. It is important for young people to look ahead and consider where they would like their careers to take them in the years ahead. In addition to upward promotion, one can often make valuable career changes by moving from one agency to another.

Most students who select the criminal justice profession as a career expect the work to be challenging and exciting. Some students also see working in criminal justice agencies as an opportunity to serve their communities and society. However, few students can envision the complexity of the work or the personal skills and traits that are required to fully meet today's challenges and to make a meaningful difference. The characteristics most desirable among criminal justice professionals include integrity, maturity, self-confidence, and the ability to accept and carry out responsibility. Sound interpersonal skills are also of the utmost importance for successful performance. The ability to relate well with people allows criminal justice professionals to deal effectively with individuals from all walks of life and with a wide array of problems, backgrounds, and attitudes. Professionals are also defined, in part, by their capacity to listen, understand, analyze, and make sound decisions, often while under pressure. These traits and skills are representative of the "select few" who can create sense out of confusion, bring order to chaos, and remain under control when others are out of control.

Many of the personal characteristics and capabilities necessary to becoming a professional cannot be taught, but rather, must be learned through life experiences. Learning from life experiences will take place only through a person's honest self-assessment in response to personal successes and failures. It is important to seek feedback from mentors, friends, or peers who are valued in order to obtain an honest self-assessment of one's life skills. Through such appraisal, we come to learn that we are indebted to many for our successes and solely responsible for our failures.

For criminal justice professionals today, and more so in the future, there are a vast number of skills that can be taught and need to be learned. To begin with, one must be able to write clear and accurate reports. Poorly written reports may allow guilty suspects to go free, can generate lawsuits, and will damage the reputation of their authors. Also, critical and logical thinking teaches students to examine all issues and assumptions, to look for facts, and to make sound judgments based upon information. The need to be bilingual is also important, especially for law enforcement officers in multi-ethnic communities. In addition, basic computer skills are a requisite for daily communications and record keeping in almost all criminal justice agencies. Moreover, advanced technological capabilities are necessary for tracking crime and investigating the growing range of offenses committed with computers. Most of these skills can be taught in college classes or training academies. But learning can only take place through commitment, personal discipline, and constant practice on the part of individuals who strive for excellence in their work.

A more recent development affecting law enforcement and the justice system is the war on international terrorism, which is predicted to last for the next two decades. As a result, criminal justice professionals will need to understand the history and culture of a number of recent immigrant ethnic groups from which terrorists may originate. Local law enforcement officers especially will have to build relationships with leaders and community members. Partnerships with citizens representing various ethnic groups will be critical to obtaining information and weeding out terrorists while protecting the safety and rights of the groups' law abiding members.

There is much to be learned on the path to professionalism. Professionals in any field consistently learn as part of their work. Continued learning promotes career growth, which is intrinsically enriching. Continuous development of professional traits and skills will lead to excellence in performance. Excellence in one's work leads to personal pride, which, in turn, makes work a joy. It all begins by carefully thinking about and planning one's career. In that regard, this book will assist you in considering your many choices.

David Kalinich
Chair, Department of Criminology and Criminal Justice
Florida Atlantic University
Boca Raton, Florida

Acknowledgments

The AUTHOR GRATEFULLY acknowledges Dr. Jeanne B. Stinchcomb, author of *Corrections Today: 21st Century Challenges*, (Prentice-Hall, 2002), for preparing portions of this manuscript.

1

Overview of Law Enforcement and Criminal Justice

When one views the history of the American police establishment, it is clear that this complex system emerged from circumstances very different from today's mobile and industrialized urban communities. Originally the English system encouraged mutual responsibility and even was known as the mutual pledge system. The phrase "hue and cry" became a familiar one as citizens were alerted to their personal responsibility for preservation of the peace. As time went on, the family grouping known as the "hundred" arose, and out of that era came the constable, whose primary duties related to custody of horses and weapons. Then several hundreds merged themselves into shires, forming the office of Shire-Reeve. This office, appointed by the crown to keep peace and order, is the source of our modern term "sheriff."

In 1066, William the Conqueror invaded England. Most historians refer to this period as a critical one in legal developments. The philosophy of an enforcement unit separate from the judiciary evolved during this time.

By the late 1200s, England had created a "watch and ward" system for fire protection, guarding the town gate, and nighttime security. Over time, the constable gained acceptance, and for centuries he was to serve as a "conservator" or peacekeeper under the justice of the peace.

Gradually, the concept of assigning landowners the responsibility of keeping the king's law gave way to taxation for the purpose of paying men who served as enforcers. In 1777, under King George III, wages were established from taxes, relieving merchants and landowners of the financial burden of law enforcement. Also, by this time, law enforcement had become a demanding task because of the pressures of the Industrial Revolution. The rural-to-urban migration that accompanied the revolution and the mob violence that led to use of military force paved the way for legislation clearly identifying the civil police.

Many law enforcement experiments before 1820 failed because no system could reconcile individual freedom of action with security of person and property. It remained for Sir Robert Peel, England's Home Secretary, in 1829, to introduce into Parliament the Act for Improving the Police In and Near the Metropolis. This led to the first organized British metropolitan police force, which was structured along military lines and numbered one thousand men. These bobbies, despite low pay, recruitment problems, and resistance from Parliament, proved so effective that similar units were established throughout England, and by 1856 Parliament had provided for every borough and county to have a police force.

The Peelian Act of 170 years ago set forth principles that are still pertinent today, and they are listed here because they remain basic tenets of the law enforcement profession:

- The police must be stable, efficient, and organized along military lines.
- The police must be under governmental control.
- The absence of crime will best prove the efficiency of police.
- The distribution of crime news is essential.
- The deployment of police strength, both by time and area, is essential.
- No quality is more indispensable to a police officer than a perfect command of temper; a quiet, determined manner has more effect than violent action.
- Good appearance commands respect.
- The securing and training of proper persons is at the root of efficiency.
- Public security demands that every police officer must be given a number.
- Police headquarters should be centrally located and easily accessible.
- Police should be hired on a probationary basis.
- Police records are necessary for the correct distribution of police strength.

Origin and Growth in America

American colonists in the seventeenth and eighteenth centuries brought to America the law enforcement structure with which they were familiar in England. The transfer of the offices of constable and sheriff to rural American areas—which included most colonial territory—was accomplished with little change in the structure of the offices.

Generally speaking, the constable became responsible for law enforcement in the towns, while the sheriff took responsibility for the counties. Also, many colonial cities adopted the night-watch system; Boston, as early as 1636, had night watchmen. The New York night watchmen were sometimes known as the "rattle watch" because they carried rattles on their rounds. Gradually, as in England, American cities began to develop their own police forces. Although Philadelphia established such a force in 1833, the ordinance was repealed several years later. In 1838 Boston created a day force to reinforce its night watch. In 1844 the New York legislature passed a law creating the first twenty-four-hour organization, and following that model, most major cities unified their day and night forces until by 1870, all cities had full-time police departments. During the remainder of the nineteenth century, a number of efforts were made to reform and improve policing both in the city and in the rural areas. Civil service enactment proved helpful, and some forces moved gradually to merit employment and less political interference. Police training schools emerged in the early 1900s, and, although quite modest, they set a standard that by the mid-twentieth century had become generally accepted.

During the 1920s came the prophetic leadership of Chief August Vollmer at Berkeley; he advertised in the University of California's student newspaper for young men to serve on the police department while obtaining their college education. Vollmer's criteria for selection were simple and direct: "high intelligence, sound nerves, good physique, sterling character, fast reaction time, good memory, and the ability to make accurate observations and correct decisions."

In 1965 the International Association of Chiefs of Police Advisory Council on Police Education and Training assembled a group of national authorities under a Ford Foundation Grant. This pioneering group stated that, ". . . generally, it is conceded that today's law enforcement officer has a need for higher education. It is also generally agreed that within the next few years, law enforcement officers will find higher education imperative."

This observation is the result of consideration of the changes that society has and is experiencing in such areas as the population explosion, the growing pressure for education beyond high school, the changing nature of metropolitan areas, and the effects of tensions and pressures ranging from automation to race relations. The law enforcement officer is required to meet all kinds of people and innumerable kinds of situations; he or she must therefore:

1. be equipped to make good value judgments,
2. be able to maintain perspective,
3. be able to understand underlying causes of human behavior,
4. be able to communicate clearly and precisely,
5. possess leadership qualities and make decisions, and
6. be knowledgeable of job skills.

In view of changing conditions that require flexibility, basic theory, and broad understanding, we can conclude that a wide spectrum of higher education must be available.

Policing in America in the 1990s and 2000s

Legal and procedural complexities have increased so much that police officers are expected to have significant knowledge of court decisions regarding searches and seizures, frisks and inquiries, arrests, and use of force. Consequently, they also have the difficult burden of having to make such decisions on the spot without benefit of analysis and discussion. Officers must also recognize and understand a body of professional knowledge that has emerged from sociology and psychology, but which is more appropriately referred to as human relations, crisis intervention, and behavioral management. Community policing and problem-oriented policing are replacing reactive responses to citizen calls for a police presence. A recent reincarnation of walking beats and bicycle patrols has emerged within neighborhood-oriented policing.

Officers also note an increased need to become better generalists on a number of matters relating to safety, threats, hazards, and crime prevention that previously had not been demanded of all police officers.

In addition, technology has become widespread and is having more impact upon policing than ever was imagined a few decades ago. This has resulted in the use of more scientific techniques to plot incidents and occurrences, to examine evidence, to collect and assess data, and to aid in mapping and predicting events. Although instrumentation, computers, and other technical devices may help make obtaining results easier and faster, street officers still increasingly need to control and manage these devices, as well as interpret their outputs for effective action.

The hard issues of years gone by, such as the role of police officers as crime fighters versus their role as community service agents, may not yet be totally resolved; however, the challenge from the community will continue to be very real and extremely conflicting at times. The more one can become educated for such a career, the better, although that alone will not resolve the dilemma created by a financially pinched community demanding better protection and greater crime prevention efforts from its police department.

Among the improvements that have been underway throughout the police service are more advanced management techniques, wider use of computer assistance, more attention to performance evaluations, and considerable attention to training needs at all levels throughout one's career. In addition, departmental policies have begun to reflect public expectations and proper police procedures.

The 1980s witnessed improved professional status for the police officer in America. Educational requirements, communication skills, sophisticated training, and technological support enlarged the position and considerably enhanced the image of the police officer. It is indisputable that the police are on the cutting edge of curtailing violence and disorder and that they must possess the skills and judgment to confront these matters effectively. The physician does this in the emergency room of a hospital; so must the police officer make wise decisions quickly and under much pressure. By the 1990s the concept of community policing had taken hold. Using a variety of techniques, the implementation of problem-solving policing and neighborhood-based policing had become widespread and generally accepted. The new century began with challenges regarding global terrorism threats and a wartime environment. Once again, more will be expected of our hometown security forces, and the American police will meet those expectations. This book is about how one can become a part of this vital enterprise.

Personnel Needs

Few occupations in the public service field offer as challenging and varied a career as law enforcement. Whether at the federal, state, or local level, employment opportunities continue to grow because of population expansion, social complexities, and governmental priorities. Undoubtedly the police of the world have emerged from a history of uncertainty as to their proper functions, but in the United States, as representatives of all citizens, they are responsible for maintaining peace and order within the framework of the law. The police role continues to advance and is enjoying greater occupational stature and prestige than ever before.

In years past, requirements for police officers, also called peace officers, were not as rigid. The service has not always effectively competed for educated young people. More recently, partly because of community concern about crime and disorder, law enforcement finds itself enjoying professional status, and its career appeal has increased among young Americans. The urgency and importance of policing is described by the President's Commission on Law Enforcement and Administration of Justice in its special *Task Force Report [on the] Police*. These important words bear repeating in this text for those considering such a career:

> The police . . . are the part of the criminal justice system that is in direct daily contact both with crime and with the public. The entire system—courts and corrections as well as the police—is charged with enforcing the law and maintaining order. What is distinctive about the responsibility of the police is that they are charged with performing these functions where all eyes are upon them and where the going is roughest, on the street.

According to U.S. Bureau of Justice Statistics, there are more than 13,500 local police departments at the city, township, and municipal levels of government. Surprising to many Americans, and most certainly amazing to foreigners, is that three-fourths of those departments operate with fewer than twenty-five sworn officers.

Looking at this same statistic from other viewpoints, about 8 percent of the sheriffs' departments employ more than one hundred sworn deputies. Of the nation's local police departments, some 15 percent have between twenty-five and one hundred sworn officers, and actually less than 1 percent of either local police or sheriff's departments have five hundred or more officers. In other words, policing in America is very much a function of local communities and modest-sized organizations.

In 2000 there were an estimated 926,583 employees, including 654,601 sworn officers, in local police and sheriffs' departments. The overall law enforcement employment rate was 3.5 per 1,000 inhabitants; but only a 2.5 rate when considering full-time sworn officers. Viewed another way, fewer than 1 million police employees administer protective services to the nation's 265 million inhabitants.

There are sometimes recommendations to consolidate some of the smaller departments, often through a contract with other larger communities or the sheriff's agency. In fact, in the past several years, the actual number of very small municipal police agencies has declined somewhat because of an increase in contractual arrangements, consolidation efforts, and other attempts to streamline and economize the numbers of different organizations. On the other hand, a community may elect to become a separate governmental unit and thus may desire its own police, in which case new departments emerge. Some of the nonmunicipal departments would include the county police agencies found in some states, housing and port authorities, townships, special districts, and school districts. Even park police may be a separate and special unit. In addition to the county sheriffs, there are forty-nine independent cities that have a sheriff because of a consolidated city-county form of government. Colleges and universities may operate their own police.

It should be noted that some county police departments are among the largest police organizations. Some examples are the Los Angeles Sheriff's Office with 7,000 sworn; Miami-Dade County Police (Florida) with 3,000; Nassau County, New York, with 3,000; Cook County, Illinois, with 2,600; and Baltimore County, Maryland, with 1,700. Likewise, 2,600 are employed in Harris County, Texas.

Further examples of the total sworn-officer strengths in some major cities will help demonstrate how large local police departments can be. By far, the largest American police agency is in New York City, where the Housing Police Authority, the Transit Police, and the local department all combine to total some 40,000 officers. These personnel cover subways, housing developments, the boroughs, and the parks. Chicago has 13,600 sworn at this writing. Los Angeles City Police has more than 9,000 officers, Philadelphia has 7,000, Houston has 5,400, and Detroit almost 4,200. Those city departments that show a sworn staff of more than 2,000 include Washington, D.C., with 3,600; Baltimore with 3,100; and Dallas with 2,800. Surrounding that 2,000-officer figure, one finds Phoenix with 2,600, Boston with 2,200, San Francisco with 2,200, Honolulu with 2,100, Cleveland with 1,900, Denver with 1,500, St. Louis with 1,500, and Kansas City with 1,250. Some very large cities, like New York and Chicago, have had even more officers, but as municipal budget reductions result in losses of personnel, the numbers of police may change as cost pressures mount in competition with crime, social disorders, and citizen fears. For purposes of this discussion, however, it should be noted that when a large community reduces its police strength, citizens eventually challenge that decision, and the organization is again increased through political authorization.

What figures such as these say to the person seeking a career in police work is that opportunities exist throughout the nation, but greater numerical vacancies will be found in the larger cities and heavily populated suburban counties that often surround the large cities. Some thirty-four departments have more than one thousand officers. However, not everyone wishes to work in the heart of urban sprawl.

Many people prefer working in the communities other than the very largest urban complexes. For these people, the options are many. Middle-range cities have police departments numbering 1,000 or more. For example, as of the latest data, Columbus, Ohio, reports 1,800 sworn officers; New Orleans 1,650; Jacksonville, Florida, 1,600; Atlanta 1,400; Seattle 1,300; and Cincinnati, Ohio, 1,000 officers.

The sworn law enforcement employment rate has increased to 3.7 percent in cities of 1,000,000 or more inhabitants when we consider the total personnel data. Suburban county agencies averaged 2.6 sworn employees per 1,000 inhabitants.

Furthermore, it should also be understood that civilian employment within law enforcement has been increasing and takes on more importance each year as agencies consider the role of the sworn officer and the tasks that nonsworn, civilian-status personnel can perform. In 1973 civilians made up 14.6 percent of all police personnel. By the 1987 data, civilians made up 25 percent of the total law enforcement employee force. The 1993 data indicated that civilians comprised 28 percent of employees. For 2000, civilians made up 30 percent. That dramatic increase over the recent decades suggests some noticeable alterations of the police work setting. It is clear evidence, too, that the more modern agencies have determined that sworn officers are not needed behind desks, but out in public providing direct services to the community. Many civilian personnel are assigned to records, communication units, labs, computers, and planning and research. They often handle citizen calls for assistance that do not involve arrests; they may also be found investigating traffic accidents or taking routine reports of a nonemergency nature. In general this suggests greater effort at productivity by moving nonenforcement duties away from sworn officers. The message seems clear that one might consider working for a police department, but in a civilian capacity. For the rural law enforcement agencies, the civilian figure is 38 percent, again demonstrating a strong commitment to civilianize much of the work of our suburban police.

Nationwide, the 1993 data indicating number of female officers remained steady—at about the 10 percent level—throughout the 1990s. In other words, male officers still dominate by 90 percent the sworn positions across the country. Women are slightly less likely to police in the rural areas—only 8 percent—but in the suburban (county) agencies they are at 13 percent.

In Los Angeles, a forerunner in the employment of women officers, the number has reached about 14 percent, with many women now in supervisory ranks and some in command ranks. Much national media publicity has been given to several cities where women have reached the top executive level and served as chief of police. The progress for women in law enforcement has been consistent and will likely continue as the nation's workforce changes and attitudes are similarly modified.

There are cities where the figure is higher because they have sought to employ women over a period of time and have distributed assignments on an equitable basis. Some of the noteworthy cities in this regard have been Washington, D.C.; Miami; New York City; Atlanta; Indianapolis, Indiana; and Detroit. Madison, Wisconsin, may hold the original record for gender equity, since 25 percent of that police department were women, even a few years ago. And among the nation's largest cities, Detroit had topped the list with 19 percent being female. However, a more recent survey placed Philadelphia at the top with nearly 25 percent female officers. A close second was Chicago with 22 percent females. In certain large cities, where the strong equal employment efforts have been concentrated, the hiring of female officers will be much greater.

When one looks to the smaller cities and small towns this figure decreases, but interestingly, increases again for rural and suburban counties, reflecting opportunities in county police and sheriff's departments. It should be pointed out for those not interested in sworn positions that the female employment percentages in all agencies for civilian jobs are significantly higher, as much as 63 percent nationally.

In addition to careers at the local level, data now indicate that over 20 percent of military police officers are female. Likewise, agencies such as the FBI and the Secret Service have recruited women for more than a decade now. The earliest state police units to recruit women include Pennsylvania and Maryland. Young women interested in police careers should seek out and speak with those who have achieved this career goal. *Breaking & Entering: Policewomen on Patrol*, by Susan E. Martin (published by the University of California, Berkeley Press, paperback, 1982), is a book highly recommended for those who wish to locate a detailed study of this subject. Another valuable resource is *The Status of Women in Policing*, also by Susan E. Martin (Police Foundation Report, Washington, D.C., 1990).

Future Outlook

New appointments must continue as estimates consistently place the number of entry-level positions available at a rather consistent thirty thousand. Some others view this as a conservative estimate based upon traditional population and economic growth projections, to say nothing of the federal government's assistance in hiring more police. The rise in crime, violence, and the public and political concern for public safety as the population grows, in both number and age, will continue to dictate a positive employment situation for jobs in police work. Retirements of those who entered in the post–World War II period are long over, those with Korean conflict duty have now served out their twenty-five- or thirty-year careers, and those retiring from Vietnam-era duty continue. Governmental budget tightening and reduced population expansion must be balanced against the personnel turnover and the demands for new services. The tug of war continues between budget tightening and demands to do more with less on the one hand, and the threats of drug abuse, international terrorism, and hazardous materials concerns, mixed with increasing support for community policing, on the other. It is even now too early to really predict the impact upon policing of such issues as airport security and demands for greater police presence on college campuses, special events, and settings that attract large crowds.

The United States Department of Labor's *Occupational Outlook Handbook* states that the kinds of police jobs that arise in the future are likely to be affected to a considerable degree by the changes now taking place in enforcement methods, strategies, and equipment. Specialists are becoming more and more essential, and there will be a greater need for officers with training ranging from engineering techniques applied to traffic control, to social work techniques applied to crime prevention, dispute resolution, and assistance for victims. Furthermore, as statistical analysis and data utilization increase, there are expanding needs for computer technicians, crime and incident data analysts, mapping specialists, and long-range planners. In addition, such concepts as the state specialist, recommended by the National Advisory Commission on Criminal Justice Standards and Goals, will enhance career opportunities in this field. All states have developed state investigative specialty units to assist local law enforcement agencies with crimes that require special investigative knowledge. The majority of these programs have been implemented for such specific societal problems as organized crime, arson, consumer protection violations, violent hate crimes, serial murders, and even computer hackers. One seeking detailed information about jobs should consult the *Dictionary of Occupational Titles* in addition to the *Occupational Outlook Handbook* mentioned above.

In the years ahead, much greater public attention will be called to police tasks that require considerable professional skills. In the past, the many challenges facing law enforcement have not been apparent and have been little understood by the public. Police status and pay have increased significantly, and educational advancements have been remarkable. Probably no single career group in history has ever achieved so much higher education in so short a time as has the American law enforcement officer. Much of this was due to a federally funded program known as the Law Enforcement Education Program (LEEP), 1968–1980. Funds were provided through grants and loans to both pre-service and in-service personnel.

Most enforcement functions and duties cannot change overnight because the primary concern of the police is to protect the public. The police department is the twenty-four-hour agency best equipped to respond to requests for assistance. Nonetheless, many dramatic changes in assignments and procedures have occurred in recent years. Authorities generally agree that the role of the police in American society is moving rapidly toward closer involvement in community-originated programs, with greater emphasis on crime prevention, and toward eliminating social problems. Recently, the police have become particularly active in efforts aimed at specific offense reduction through programs to harden frequent targets, encourage greater use of locks and alarms, and, in general, advise home owners and the business community about crime risks. In the years ahead, the enforcement officer must display greater insight into community problems, social sciences, conflict resolutions, and the complex factors that contribute to unlawful or ill-advised activities. They are even now becoming more knowledgeable about biochemical hazards, toxic threats, diseases, and spills.

No one can predict entirely to what extent policing will change as more data become computerized and the agencies become more involved with community planning, tightened security, and crime prevention. It is always safe to assume, however, that competent personnel will be in demand and that training and education have now become an integral part of the system. Future duties and salaries of police officers are beyond our estimates today, but policing is being acknowledged as deserving of full professional recognition, with rigid state licensing for those who practice its calling. As in other professions, job descriptions will reflect a variety of tasks according to the level of career preparation.

The job is truly a fascinating one, and priorities tend to be with crime prevention, conflict resolution, tension reduction, removal of fears and threats, and a proactive effort aimed toward maintaining peace and security for all.

2

JOBS AT THE CITY AND COUNTY LEVELS

COUNSELING FOR A career choice in law enforcement varies rather extensively, depending upon the jurisdictional level that one is interested in joining. The federal agencies are easier to apply for, in the sense that a single office furnishes information and applications and affords the applicant centralized procedural steps. Likewise at the state level, whether it is a state police or a highway patrol, there would be a central headquarters responsible for all personnel matters. It is at the local level, where the greatest number of opportunities exists, that no one procedure or process is available. Once an individual has made the decision to seriously consider entering this exciting and challenging field, contact should be made with the department in which the applicant is interested to obtain its specific requirements. However, this book will attempt to describe the entrance process generally found throughout city and county police agencies.

Personal Requirements

Although it may seem a relatively simple matter, the serious applicant should not take the initial formal job application lightly. It is often designed to test one's ability to follow instructions, provide details, and be honest and thorough. The background investigation will prevail, so applicants should be complete in reporting their experiences. The best advice is not to try to hide a poor traffic record in another state or a minor involvement with authorities during teenage years. Above all, do not leave blanks on the application or fail to provide details when requested. Agencies' first impressions will be based largely upon that application form. This advice cannot be stressed enough; leave no blanks and tell the whole truth!

In addition to personal questions, a written application will contain other questions regarding relatives, friends, business references, military service, and formal schooling. Quite possibly the applicant will also be asked to state reasons for being interested in a law enforcement career with that particular organization. United States citizenship is required by all law enforcement agencies, but recently there has been some relaxation of that rule in order to accommodate permanent resident aliens, especially those who speak a needed foreign language. Some departments have eliminated prior local residency requirements of the police applicant, although by no means have they been totally removed. State residency may be required prior to employment, but the trend now is to invite applications from any area of the United States. Once hired, an employee may be required to reside within a given city or county.

In the United States, entrance age requirements now range from a minimum of 21 (in some jurisdictions, 19) to a maximum of 35 years, although some departments may hire applicants up to age 40.

In certain circumstances, high school graduates may obtain employment through a cadet program (often termed Public Service Aide or Community Services Officer). The cadet program allows individuals to be employed before their twenty-first birthday, and it also provides for consideration of employment as a police officer upon reaching the twenty-first birthday. Cadet programs have enabled young persons to become acquainted with the police field through various nonenforcement tasks. An applicant might consider making formal application prior to age 21, as the process itself takes some time, and there are departments that permit the submission of applications as much as one year in advance. Also, there are departments that allow entrance into the training program if the recruit will become 21 years old while training is in progress. Several major departments, notably Miami, Houston, Dallas, and Philadelphia, some years ago began to accept candidates under the age of 21, even authorizing them for street duty. This recruiting procedure may continue to expand, although many agency chiefs believe that 21 should be the minimum age level for police service. Also, as lateral transfers continue, there will be more opportunity to enter another department up to age 40, when the applicant has had prior police experience elsewhere.

All police departments require applicants to be of good moral character, emotionally stable, and mature. A serious or lengthy criminal record, particularly conviction, will be the basis for rejection. Serious prior traffic violations, especially as an adult, could also result in disqualification, since possession of a valid driver's license is required. All applicants are given a thorough background investigation that will determine their integrity, reliability, and sobriety. The applicant's habits, conduct, and reputation in the community will be evaluated. Additional screening may also include one or a series of psychological tests, with or without accompanying interviews. Some police departments utilize psychiatrists to test and interview applicants, but this has proven costly and no more effective than psychological assessments. A polygraph examination may be required, and a personal interview is an absolute certainty. The interview may include both individual and group meetings.

Written Tests

Written tests are common and practical because they can be easily administered and scored and are economical. Several large personnel testing firms provide specialized examinations for police applicants. During the 1970s written entrance exams were challenged legally as not being reflective of all cultures and genders, and much research has gone into making such tests job based, bias free, and universally acceptable. Thorough job-task analysis has made entrance tests widely used and generally more reliable and valid. One can definitely expect a lengthy written examination when seeking public safety employment. In fact, far more applicants take such tests than ever obtain employment, and some agencies consider the stress and experience of undergoing the test and following instructions as the first of many application hurdles to becoming an officer. Regardless of the type of written test the applicant may encounter, the following skills will always improve applicants' abilities to express themselves in writing: reading comprehension, analytical ability, self-expression, and capacity to retain details, recall events, and make decisions based upon facts.

All departments now require successful completion of high school, although various alternatives do exist, such as certification through the Armed Services Institute or equivalency examinations

(GED) by a state department of education. Some increasing numbers of agencies now require a year or more of higher education, so be sure to check on that when looking at options. Applicants are not generally required to be knowledgeable about law enforcement prior to their employment, but an applicant with advanced academic knowledge in the field may reasonably be expected to be better qualified for such employment.

Physical Examinations

Police service at any level of government requires physically sound personnel. Severe physical exertion is called for occasionally, and the applicant, male or female, must possess the stamina to work for long periods of time without rest.

Minimum medical standards have been established and are observed by most departments. Generally, any marked deformity, overweight condition, or weak muscular development may result in disqualification. Hearing and visual acuity must be within acceptable limits, although most departments permit corrective lenses to be worn. Thus far, the courts have paid little attention to standards related to vision and general physical health, since these are reasonably job related. Generally speaking, eyesight must be correctable to 20/20 and no color blindness is permitted.

Minimum height and weight requirements had become the subject of controversy, and height and weight standards are being made more flexible in order to include a more representative group of applicants. However, the medical examination still prevails and weight must be in proportion to height, although the minimum height standard has been lowered.

Of course, anyone seeking a police appointment must undergo a complete medical examination. This often is requested early in the process, since certain physical conditions do account for a significant number of rejections. Excessively high or low blood pressure, heart conditions, lack of required strength and agility, and inadequate coordination skills can all result in medical rejection. Furthermore, recent evidence of serious or prolonged drug usage will disqualify the applicant. Urinalysis will be required by most agencies to determine the current status of alcohol and drugs in the body. The more stringent agencies will require urinalysis during the medical screening, during the academy training, and perhaps following the training, prior to assignments.

Personal Interview

One almost unanimous requirement among enforcement agencies is some form of personal interview, and this can be of great importance. The interview board generally consists of several representatives from the police department, as well as someone from the personnel department of the employing jurisdiction. Interview lengths vary considerably, but the inquiries tend to revolve around the applicant's past work experience, education, personal history and characteristics, and reasons for choosing police work as a career. And applicants should bear in mind that the board not only will be judging responses to questions, but also personal appearance and manner. Of particular importance will be the applicant's expression of interest in a police career and intention to pursue it in a dedicated way.

Polygraph–Lie Detector Examinations

Over the years this particular selection technique has varied in emphasis. Presently it is widely used among agencies because of the increased illegal drug problem in the country. Typical previous use of the polygraph was limited to exploring thefts from employers, being removed from prior employment, and situations dealing with use of other's property. Currently the emphasis in polygraph examinations is on prior and continuing use of illegal drugs. The type of drug, extent of the usage, and the time interval since that usage are all factors that will be considered. The polygraph may also be used to ascertain discrepancies in time periods or for clarifying questions regarding one's personal history and involvement in previous activities.

Background Investigation

Quite understandably, all police agencies require that a character or background investigation be conducted on each applicant. This is a time-consuming and costly procedure and almost always occurs toward the end of the selection process. Thus, this effort would not be expended on applicants who had failed to qualify on previous criteria. It is important that the candidate furnish as much detail as possible so this investigation can be performed without unnecessary delays. As a brief example, the complete names, titles, addresses, and phone numbers of references should be furnished. All previous employment and residence locations must be accurate, and an applicant should remember that he or she is being evaluated by the information furnished. Failure to include all pertinent data or to account for any time periods may cause serious delay and even rejection. If an applicant spent time in the military or in college, and there are brief time intervals when neither was the primary activity, the time gap should be explained. If you believe the application process is appealing and that you can successfully meet the rather stringent requirements, then a law enforcement career may be for you. But before you decide, consider those abilities that research has established as critical to the tasks performed by police officers. Whether they are analyzed through written exams, personal and group interviews, medical analyses, psychological screening, polygraph tests, assessment center exercises, psychiatric interviews, and/or agility and motor ability demonstrations, these traits have survived the research and must be possessed by the applicant. They include:

Leadership

Initiate action and independently assume control of a situation; obtain information from others; direct, assist, and provide guidance to others.

Maturity

Display courtesy and consideration for the problems, needs, and feelings of others in a fair manner; use discretion in exercising police authority.

Perception

Identify and understand the critical elements of a situation; observe situational details and conditions; recognize discrepancies or circumstances that require action; interpret the implications of such actions.

Good Judgment

Use logical and sound judgment when responding to a situation based upon a recognition and understanding of the facts available; define problem situations and initiate actions based upon established guidelines and procedures.

Decisiveness

Willingly take action and make decisions based upon situational need; render judgments; willingly defend actions or decisions when confronted by others.

Adaptability

Be flexible when dealing with situations involving change; appropriately modify a course of action as the situation changes; maintain constructive behavior despite time pressures or pressures exerted by others.

Oral Communication

Clearly express oneself through oral means: properly used grammar, vocabulary, eye contact, and voice inflection.

Written Communication

Clearly and effectively communicate relevant information in writing; use accurate vocabulary and proper grammar and spelling.

These characteristics are the result of research conducted at the Miami-Dade (Florida) Assessment Center for entry-level police officers, which identified and grouped 102 specific skills and abilities required of the entry-level police officer.

Probation, Tenure, and Promotion

The length of the probation period after employment is usually one year, and two years at the most. After serving the probationary period successfully, the majority of departments ensure job security, except for cases in which formal charges are brought against the employee.

Very few significant differences exist among most law enforcement agencies with regard to promotion. Likewise, most agencies have a stated, formal promotion program. Generally seniority in a particular rank may be among those factors considered in promoting an employee. An oral interview also is conducted, along with an evaluation of general service experience in the department. In addition, to attain most ranks, there may well be a written examination and some type of job performance assessment. Formal performance appraisals will be conducted as often as every month or at least quarterly. Even if such personnel activity evaluations are only semi-annual, they provide valuable insights about an individual's ability to do the current job.

Performance evaluations typically review the officer's skill as measured by a number of events. These might include arrests, court convictions, persons interviewed in the course of patrol duties, cases investigated, reports filed, and numerous other categories. Any citizen complaints formally charged against the officer, and likewise any commendations, would also be considered; so might attitude, appearance, and professional demeanor. The written examination, common in most agencies, should address issues needed in the position being sought; i.e., for sergeants, the test should focus upon supervisory skills, basic managerial concepts, and other areas of agency concern such as legal procedures, community policing, or administrative knowledge.

In recent years articulate, better-educated officers have done exceptionally well in front of the oral interview board, and promotions may well continue to occur in this manner until higher education becomes an integral part of the requirements for promotion. In many of the more progressive agencies, there are now assessment centers where simulated exercises, role playing, and objective reviews that assist in the promotional process are conducted. They do not necessarily replace written examinations or oral interviews, but they are a very useful method for making impartial comparisons among candidates for a position, and they are based upon actual behavioral events, not just test scores. To the extent that the simulations are designed to resemble actual job demands and expectations, the assessment center is becoming the process for the future in selecting finalists for promotions in rank.

The Patrol Officer

Patrol is high on police management's list of priorities because most departments spend 90 percent of their budget for personnel and as much as 60 percent of their budget on patrol personnel specifically. Further strengthening the significance of patrol, the National Advisory Commission on Standards and Goals has recommended that every police administrator ensure maximum efficiency in the delivery of patrol services. This will include immediate response to incidents, an emphasis on the need for preventive patrol to reduce the opportunity for criminal activity, and priority status upon each request for police service.

Not only is patrol the backbone of the crime prevention effort, it is also the foundation of the greatest part of all community contact and communication. The patrol officer is the everyday representative of the law enforcement agencies to the community at large, and he or she has the greatest impact upon community life.

The International Association of Chiefs of Police developed the following job description for the police patrol officer:

General Duties

The patrol officer is responsible, through the enforcement of laws and ordinances, for the protection of life and property in an assigned area during a specific period. He or she performs routine police assignments received from officers of superior ranks, conducts preliminary investigations, and assists in the apprehension of criminals. The patrol officer also performs special assignments requiring specialized skills or abilities.

Distinguishing Features of the Class

This work consists primarily of routine patrol tasks. Work may include elements of danger and does involve many emergencies that require an employee to exercise sound judgment and act without direct supervision. However, procedures and special assignments are usually carried out under immediate supervision.

The patrol officer may perform any or all of the following duties:

- patrols a specific area typically in a patrol car to preserve law and order, to prevent and discover the commission of crime, and to enforce parking and traffic regulations
- is required to make close inspection of actual or potential hazards to the public safety
- responds to complaints concerning automobile crashes, robberies, and other minor and major violations of law
- interviews persons making complaints and inquiries and attempts to make proper disposition or direct them to proper authorities
- investigates suspicious activities and makes arrests for violations of federal and state laws and local ordinances

- watches for and makes investigations of wanted and missing persons and stolen cars and property
- conducts preliminary investigations
- administers first aid at the scenes of accidents and crimes
- maintains order in crowds
- answers questions and directs the public
- performs periodic safety and crime prevention tasks as community requirements dictate
- ensures the rights of all citizens are protected and intervenes in disputes and disturbances to reduce their risk of becoming a crisis

The patrol officer is also required to possess the following knowledge, skills, and abilities:

- good general intelligence and emotional stability
- good judgment
- ability to analyze situations quickly and objectively and to determine the necessary and proper action
- ability to understand and carry out complex oral and written directions
- good powers of observation and memory
- ability to compose and legibly write or print complete factual reports
- a good knowledge of first aid methods, after training
- ability to speak effectively
- ability to drive a car safely
- excellent moral character
- excellent physical condition
- physical endurance and agility
- skill in the use and handling of firearms, after training

The Job Description

As indicated in the President's Commission on Law Enforcement and Administration of Justice in the special *Task Force Report [on the] Police*, an officer patrols a particular area or neighborhood on foot or by vehicle. While on patrol, safe response to calls for assistance from the general public is a primary responsibility. These calls may be initiated from police headquarters or directly by a citizen. In either case, what the police officer does after arriving at the scene depends largely upon what has happened and how much information is available at that moment.

First the officer may find it necessary to hear a report from the victim of a crime or accident or from witnesses who observed the incident. The next course of action may be placing someone under arrest or entering the information obtained into a report for later investigation. Depending on the situation, the patrol officer may be called upon to preserve the peace through some immediate action or observe some piece of evidence that must be safeguarded and recorded. If an arrest is made, the suspect must be transported to the police station for the booking process. Enforcement personnel also assist the injured citizen in making a formal complaint. In the more serious cases, duties will include not only protecting the scene of the crime and obtaining information from witnesses, but also telling the investigators how the crime occurred and giving them any available clues.

In the case of a traffic crash, the police officer's duties involve rendering first aid, calling for an ambulance, preventing further damage, noting all pertinent facts, and obtaining statements from those involved as well as any witnesses. Of course, all of these matters necessitate a detailed recording and reporting of events.

The officer must also provide assistance in times of emergency such as fires or other catastrophes. Police assistance is not only sought during major calamities; it may consist of hundreds of requests for miscellaneous services: a domestic animal in trouble, a citizen in some distress, a lost child or elderly person, or such lost property as a bicycle, purse, or pet.

Often the police officer finds it necessary to issue traffic citations according to the motor vehicle code in the locale. Some violations may demand physical arrests, and, again, all will require full reporting of the action taken. The matter of driving under the influence of alcohol or drugs has taken on many new dimensions in recent years.

A great deal of time is devoted to observing and noting circumstances that could lead to more serious situations. Here the officer must identify potential hazards, whether they be neglect of children, the breeding of locations of unlawful behaviors, dangers to the personal safety of citizens, or any other conditions that might erupt into crime, disorder, or violence. Business locations also are inspected to reduce the likelihood of burglaries. Community styled policing measures have added duties that are more proactive for the common good, and they make today's officer more attuned to citizen needs and fears and less reliant on the police radio for all the daily assignments.

As one can readily see, not as much time is spent by police in making arrests, but once an arrest is made, it is necessary for the officer to appear in court. This calls for preparing notes and testimony that are accurate and relevant to the case. The officer must repeat conversations accurately and introduce exhibits and evidence in a professional, competent manner.

One of the most sensitive of the tasks that must be performed is the use of physical force to restrain someone who may assault an officer or another citizen. The patrol officer must always be prepared to repel violent assaults with proficient defensive tactics or the use of weapons, and he or she must also stay alert to prevent the escape of persons in custody. The use of nonlethal weapons now makes this task less deadly than it has been in the past.

Standard equipment for most police patrols in our country includes automobiles. A single uniformed officer in a marked patrol car is a familiar sight to everyone. Some circumstances demand that two officers ride patrol together, and communities generally find a combination of one- and two-officer vehicles to be the most appropriate policy. Few state police or deputy sheriffs patrol in pairs, but municipal officers handling numerous drunken, fighting, or domestic violence calls find it advantageous.

In recent years, the motorized scooter has become useful in traffic work because it gets the police officer to the scene rapidly, unhampered by street congestion. Equipped with a walkie-talkie radio, the officer on a scooter is frequently in a position to confront a holdup or assault in progress.

Naturally, all of these methods may be used in varying degrees, depending upon the size of the community and demands made upon the department. The person who has chosen a police career can expect to spend much time in automobile patrol, but alternatives do exist. Flexibility is essential in delivering services to the public, and this variation holds great appeal for many. In helicopters, in patrol boats, sometimes working with canine units, and occasionally still on horseback, patrol officers pursue their missions of enforcing laws, protecting citizens and their property, preventing crime and disorder, and ensuring the peace.

A police career aspirant should bear in mind that the daily work schedule will differ somewhat from that of neighbors and friends. It must be recognized that patrol is a twenty-four-hour-a-day activity, that it cannot be reduced on holidays or weekends and, further, that many serious occurrences arise in the late evening and early morning hours. Beyond this, it must also be remembered that because an officer is always a sworn protector of law and order, on-duty status is never really abandoned. One is subject to the call to duty at any time and to overtime and extended shifts, and most enforcement personnel must devote a large amount of their time to completing the necessary reports and appearing in court.

Thus a tour of duty on patrol may close without headlines and may be relatively routine, but to the officer it may include hidden dangers, suspense, monotony, and a few moments of tension and excitement. An unpredictable time, such as a quiet Sunday morning, can bring holdup and homicide.

As we observed earlier, a few major changes have occurred in the basic patrol functions in modern times: technology has improved, record systems are rapid, and the training available to officers has increased immensely. But patrol still entails covering one's assigned area, preventing crime, and providing service. Officers today are more aware of constitutional rights, legitimate dissent, and the varied implications of taking official action, but the fundamental responsibilities have not changed.

Foot patrol has also been shown to reduce citizen fear and improve relationships between police and communities. In many communities, after decades of automobile patrol coverage, the police are returning to foot patrol. Foot patrol also shows evidence of increasing officers' satisfaction with their work because they are able to demonstrate reduction in certain crimes.

The 1990s have shown us that community policing will survive. It is quite a different approach from the traditional one of efficient response to all needs. It is not incident or technology driven; officers are decentralized and must be in contact with citizens. It allocates police on the basis of neighborhoods, rather than being on-call and in-service to respond to anything.

Body armor has been introduced, vehicles are safer and more efficient, minicomputers can now deliver answers to field officers, and today's average police officer enjoys some distinct personal advantages in salary progression, benefits, and technical support. Nonetheless the job still demands intensity and alertness, and officers continue to find that violent crime-fighting duties consume far less time than do the service and protection functions that occupy their normal working hours.

Now that we have discussed in some detail the duties of the patrol officer, let us turn our attention to certain other categories of departmental assignments. Although one may seek or request certain types of assignments, it must always be remembered that the needs of the community, and the priorities of the agency, must come first. There is no real rule of thumb when it comes to specialized duty assignments: some are long-term by mutual agreement, some are short-term for a variety of reasons. But in nearly all instances, experience is a factor that remains important. Performance, of course, is another.

The Traffic Officer

The officer assigned to the traffic division or traffic bureau spends considerable time directing and controlling the flow of traffic. This function includes both motor vehicles and pedestrians. In addition to the traffic flow, the officer must be concerned with enforcing parking regulations, although sometimes this is handled by parking enforcement specialists, police cadets, or a specialized unit within the traffic division. Stolen or wanted automobiles are an important part of this unit's total responsibilities, and many such cars are located as a result of relatively minor traffic violations.

The traffic officer frequently is responsible for investigation of abandoned automobiles, as well as their removal. As in the traffic engineering division, reports must be made on the breakdown or inefficiency of traffic control devices.

A very important function of the police traffic specialist relates to the investigation of accidents. Not only must first aid be administered at the scene, but the traffic officer's reports also are critical to explaining the causes of accidents and recommending any corrections that might be necessary to prevent future crashes. This may include such things as sign dimensions, obstructions to vision, engineering hazards, or driver inattention and bad habits.

The task of issuing traffic citations and making arrests of serious violators belongs to the entire police department, but traffic officers, particularly those on motorcycles, tend to give this greater priority. As in all other police assignments, the traffic enforcement officer spends time testifying in court and frequently becomes involved in civil cases arising out of traffic accidents. Motorist assistance, escort duty, crowd handling, and rerouting traffic all place great time demands on those officers concerned with traffic and highway safety. Traffic enforcement that is fair and efficient is very important in permitting all citizens to go about their daily routines.

The Detective or Criminal Investigator

Detective work in municipal departments typically begins where the activities of the patrol personnel end. It involves the continuation of investigations, apprehension of any offenders who have been identified, recovery of stolen properties, and, again, the important tasks of completing official reports and preparing testimony and evidence for court presentation. Detectives do all follow-up interviewing because the preliminary information-gathering process may have unconnected points in it and may require analysis that cannot be done easily at the initial scene by the patrol officer.

Another critical task confronting the detective is the identification of the offender. This demands that one spend considerable time reviewing physical evidence, clues, interviews, files, background details of the event, and the offender's method of operation, with the ultimate goal of obtaining identification.

In many ways the detective is a coordinator of investigations, utilizing the efforts of the patrol officers, laboratory personnel, computerized data and records, and affected citizens in the quest for accurate information.

Insofar as property is concerned, the detective must obtain a detailed inventory of all stolen items, including serial numbers, labels, markings, and any other distinctive data. The job of recovery requires contact with pawnshops and junkyards, as well as a few persons in the community who make their living through selling stolen articles. These people are popularly referred to as "fences," and they often operate behind legitimate businesses.

Most detectives are assigned to that position, and departmental policy determines whether it is temporary or permanent. In some departments the detective status is acquired through examination, in addition to impressive performance as a patrol officer. Sometimes detectives are rotated back to the patrol unit, and in some departments detective status is regarded as a promotion, thus becoming a permanent assignment, at least until the officer is promoted to a higher rank.

Any successful detective must possess these traits: energy, persistence, courage, initiative, resourcefulness, imagination, accurate
memory, good judgment, and powers of observation. Some of
these qualities may be gained through training and experience;
others are an integral part of one's personality.

As a general rule, detectives specialize in certain kinds of
offenses: crimes against persons, such as assault, homicide, rape,
and robbery; and those against property, notably burglary, theft,
and larceny. Detectives may likewise be assigned to juvenile delinquency and youth crimes or to handling gangs and school-related
offenses. There are also criminal investigative specialists in such
technical areas as arson, auto theft, forgery, fraud, narcotics, and
the more frequent illegal activities associated with vices (for example, gambling, prostitution, and illegal beverages). Consumer
fraud, computer crimes, and hate crimes all represent some of the
newer violations that investigators must confront.

Such assignments involve long hours and demand patient and
tireless effort, but they also carry with them a somewhat higher pay
scale, a clothing allowance, more flexible working hours, and greater
freedom of activity. Also, the detective usually acquires a prestige
that is especially attractive to young, ambitious patrol officers.

Team policing, the use of targeted patrol, and other modern
approaches to better manpower utilization have attempted to combine the patrol function with that of the detective. Police departments are performing combined functions within a specific
geographic area in this way by increasing employee responsibility
and demanding accountability. Small groups of personnel enhance
the opportunity for individual officer decision making, enabling
many departments to obtain better citizen cooperation and mini-

mize the complexities of large organizations and mobile societies. For the educated officer the challenge is greater, since more personal autonomy can be exerted.

In the recent past much study and analysis has been conducted regarding how criminal investigations are prioritized and managed. Some agencies now use the patrol officer to a greater extent in the preliminary investigation, and even during follow-up work when it involves witnesses, records and files originating with the patrol officer, and informants. Future strategies will likely call for more targeted investigations in which cases are carefully screened, some are given priority, resources are more carefully managed, and emphasis is placed upon known, serious, and repeat offenders. A recent federal study provides insight for future policy making by indicating that most robbery and burglary investigations are solved equally by criminal investigators and patrol officers, that such cases are conducted in a relatively short time span, that leads tend to dissolve after several days, and that the best sources of information are witnesses, informants, police records, and other police officers.

In addition to the areas of specialty already mentioned, the size and demands of the agency will dictate the need for any others.

Specialized Assignments

The following are some of the specialized assignments required in modern police service:

- *Bomb and arson officers* use specialized equipment and training to detect and disarm explosives or suspicious devices. They also investigate fires when the origin is in question.

- *Canine officers* are teamed with specially trained dogs to provide special skills in searches, tracking, and crowd control. Canine patrol units are in common use everywhere, locating everything from bodies, to bombs, to persons hiding during chases.
- *Community relations officers* maintain contact and relationships between the police department and the community they serve. They are instrumental in crime prevention efforts and may provide links to schools, civic groups, and businesses as a part of their crime reduction and personal safety programs. School resource officers may be in this type of unit.
- *Emergency services or tactical units* are specially trained to perform rescues of various kinds. They are called to the scene of life-threatening events and have special equipment to facilitate their work. Special weapons and tactics teams support patrol units. Sometimes these units are referred to as special operations, special response, or special weapons teams.
- *Harbor patrol, helicopter, and short takeoff and landing aircraft* are all a part of modern patrol work. Duties of those on such assignments will range from distress and rescue calls to pursuit of smugglers and observation of ground activities for both safety and surveillance missions.
- *Anticrime or street crime units* work in high-crime areas and specialize in overt efforts to fight aggressive street crime. They may employ decoy tactics, stakeouts, or high visibility. Some may be assigned to gang control. Some may serve on the robbery reduction or violent crime task force.
- *Specialty units* may exist for such purposes as dealing with juveniles and youths, sex crimes, alcohol and narcotics

offenses, or any other criminal activities that require special attention. In recent years, drug abuse has compounded workloads.

- Additionally, there are assignments to hostage negotiation teams, organized crime sections, intelligence gathering, as well as internal affairs. And for those with the proper educational credentials, the training center or the academy staff may be a viable and most rewarding assignment.

When one considers further the potential for duty assignments to the training academy, property control, records and identification, laboratory with mobile units, and numerous other less recognized but highly demanding areas of responsibility, it is easier to understand why law enforcement is regarded as a diverse and challenging occupation. Police agencies have legal advisors, researchers, data analysts, forensic scientists, computer programmers, and personnel specialists, some of whom could be police officers with long-term career assignments. Some of these could be civilians, too. A profile of the police would show a typical distribution similar to the following:

- 75 percent of all sworn personnel are line/patrol officers.
- 13 percent are management and command-level officers.
- 12 percent are first-line supervisors, typically sergeants.

County Units and Sheriffs' Departments

Law enforcement career seekers may want to consider service at the county level of government. Some states have developed county-wide police units that are organized and administered similarly to city departments. In such places, patrol duties are the same as in the city department, except that the county employee may be responsible for a more extensive geographic area. Depending upon the population density, the county officer may find the duties similar to those of the state police officer. That is, a great variety of services will be performed while covering a broad geographic area, with many demands from the smaller communities and unincorporated sections. In several states, notably New York, Kentucky, Texas, Florida, Maryland, and Virginia, authorities regard certain county police departments as some of the nation's finest examples of progress in maintaining law and order.

Often regarded as models of organization and performance, these same county departments have enjoyed very progressive leadership, with chiefs being appointed by the county executive or by a county board of commissioners. County police departments are not to be confused with sheriffs' departments, although actual assignments and duties may not be very different. The sheriff is a constitutional officer and is historically and typically an elected official. The sheriff's office is found in most states where county police are not. The sheriff will possess some constitutional powers not generally assigned to the appointed police chief. Depending upon size of the population to be served, the sheriff will employ a force of uniformed deputies and, in many cases, plainclothes investigators. Since sheriffs are responsible for the administration of the county jail, they must also maintain a continuous twenty-four-hour staff in that facility.

As a general rule, the sheriff's deputies perform patrol services, investigate offenses, and provide protection in the same manner as municipal law enforcement officers. The most significant difference, other than maintaining the county jail, is the sheriff's responsibility for serving civil papers and orders of the county courts and for transporting prisoners.

In recent years, sheriffs' departments have been able to move away from their historical fee system and adopt salary scales that are usually competitive with those of colleagues in the major cities. More recently, the sheriffs have been able to secure civil service coverage for many of their employees, and while the sheriffs themselves must run for office in a popular election, many have succeeded in securing job protection for their deputies.

Like the state police officer, the deputy sheriff can expect to be confronted by a variety of demands. Because such officers usually patrol alone, they must demonstrate resourcefulness and leadership. Deputy sheriffs are very much like their municipal counterparts; the significant difference lies in the organization and the jurisdiction of the agency itself.

With regard to the differences, deputy sheriffs often serve in the courtroom as bailiffs. They also may act as extradition officers for prisoner escorts and serve orders or civil papers of the county court, including subpoenas, show-cause orders, property seizures, and garnishments. Some deputies are responsible for collecting legal fees assigned by the courts, some have jurisdiction in county parks and game areas, and, currently, many have duty protecting court facilities and court officials. Some of the sheriffs' departments that employ patrol services have contracted with smaller units of government, perhaps a township, and provide the police services for that community on the basis of the contract. In a circumstance such as this, often considered to be a progressive and productive arrangement, opportunities for employment may often increase, although there may be fewer police agencies in the area.

One seeking a law enforcement career should certainly not overlook the many townships, boroughs, villages, and modest-sized cities that dominate this nation. Although this book tends to cite illustrations and activities most often identified with the more dense populations, the role of the police does not differ much from a large urban center to a small village. The events to be responded to and the problems to be solved are often the same; what differs is the frequency with which they occur and the intensity with which the various demands arise. There are anticipated growths in personnel in many of the suburban and mid-sized towns as populations move out from the urban centers. This redistribution of police personnel is under way and promises to continue with annexations, contracting, consolidations, and rural America's insistence upon equal services.

Entrance qualifications and procedures, the desirability of higher education, the importance of training, the benefits and advantages of the job, and the potential for advancement and other careers, all will apply as much at the county level as in other areas of law enforcement. In fact, recent and rapid population movements to the suburbs, the unincorporated areas, and the smaller communities on the periphery of large cities may increase potential for employment and expanded career choices at county agencies.

3

JOBS AT THE STATE LEVEL

THE EASIEST TO recognize of the modern enforcement units may be the comparatively new state police, which has full criminal enforcement powers, or the highway patrol, which has power limited to enforcing the state's motor vehicle code. Because of their twentieth-century origin, these departments tend to be free of some of the early municipal police traditions and have generally managed to mature into well-organized, well-trained, and highly respected organizations.

Although some had modest beginnings in 1835 (Massachusetts) and in 1865 (Texas Rangers), most authors refer to 1903 in Pennsylvania as the beginning of a true statewide agency possessing full enforcement powers. Arizona in 1901 had a ranger force similar to that in Texas, Connecticut in 1903 had a force similar to that of Massachusetts, and New Mexico established mounted police in 1905. Others followed in rapid succession, and today all states except Hawaii have some statewide enforcement unit headed by a superintendent or director who is appointed by the governor.

More than half of the highway patrols and state police function as one agency within the state's Department of Public Safety. A lesser number operate as separate agencies whose chief administrators report directly to the governor. There are currently more than fifty-eight thousand sworn officers representing state police and highway patrols. Note that employment opportunities exist in state agencies beyond those with the state police or highway patrol. There are also many regulatory and specialized investigative agencies, and they, too, are included in this chapter.

State Police and Highway Patrol

All state patrol agencies require high school graduation (or the equivalent), and a number now require some college. In Florida, for example, since 1994 the highway patrol has encouraged applicants to have two years of college (sixty credits), and gives priority hiring status to those with college backgrounds. Likewise, for several years now, some other states, reaching from Delaware to Louisiana and from Texas to Illinois and Washington, have all given hiring preferences to job candidates with two or more years of higher education.

With regard to minimum age, there has been a downward trend in the last few years, and approximately one-third of these organizations permit entrance at less than twenty-one years of age. Another previous state police requirement experiencing a decline has been height, with most of the departments reporting that they no longer have a height minimum. Specific details as to physical requirements can be obtained from the headquarters unit in your state capital. In general, however, there is little difference from those characteristics described for entry into local police service.

Since both the state police and the highway patrol are quasi military units, the rank system begins with private, and, after achieving satisfactory proficiency ratings and service, the trooper can advance to private first class. Then, through written and oral examinations and maintaining satisfactory proficiency ratings, the trooper can be promoted from corporal through sergeant and into the ranks of lieutenant, captain, and so on. In almost all departments, the superintendent carries the rank of colonel.

The highway patrol enforces the Motor Vehicle Code and works primarily on state highways, interstate systems, and roads in the unincorporated areas of the counties. In some states, greater enforcement powers are being delegated to the highway patrol, as it becomes evident that the use of the automobile is associated with much of our violent crime. The state police officer, in contrast to the highway patrol, does have full police powers throughout the state, although in practice more of the work is in the unincorporated communities. In terms of the daily routine, however, the state police officer also spends considerable time enforcing the Motor Vehicle Code on the highways. Either the highway patrol or the state police can legally function where city or town police exist, but they usually do so only at the request of city officials or upon order from the governor. These requests and orders are most likely to occur during emergency situations such as natural disasters, civil disorders, or excessive criminal activities beyond the capability of the local agency.

In general, whether the highway patrol or the state police employs state officers, their training is lengthy, rigorous, and thorough. Recruits in these departments commonly undergo five to six months' training at recruit academies—during which time they receive intensive firearms and physical training, as well as instruction relating to their many enforcement responsibilities.[1] The classroom training is always supplemented with field experience, so the new trooper has considerable opportunity to practice what has been studied in the academy.[2] Some of the most rigorous law enforcement training is that experienced by the recruit state trooper, and the basic topics will usually be similar to those described for local-level police officers. The recruit trooper's day is quite similar to that of an army recruit; it begins early in the morning with physical training and continues into the evening with study and maintenance of equipment. In addition to classroom hours studying criminal law, traffic ordinances, accident investigation, and community relations, the recruit must practice pursuit driving, first aid, the use of weapons, and completing detailed reports.

As assignments of state police officers to urban settings increase, there has been a major commitment to training in human relations, citizen relationships, and interpersonal skills. In some states, recent attempts to reduce driving under the influence of alcohol and/or drugs have expanded the duties of the trooper far beyond routine patrol and accident investigation. State officers may be called upon to assist and support the local police with traffic control and enforcement or through back-up actions with full enforcement powers.

---

[1]As reported in the Comparative Data Report of the International Association of Chiefs of Police, the average number of hours spent by recruits in a training academy is 1,000 hours for highway patrols and 1,000 hours for state police departments.

[2]As also reported by the IACP, the average number of hours that recruits spend on the road in supervised field training is a minimum of 500 hours for highway patrols and 500 hours for the state police.

Although duty in the state organization may involve some transfers and reassignment to other sections of that state, there is much
to be said for the opportunities in either state police or highway
patrol units. Troopers nearly always patrol alone and, therefore,
must possess versatility and a capacity for taking full responsibility
in a critical situation. They often perform some distance away from
their headquarters and their supervisors. They must be prepared,
through temperament and training, to adapt rapidly to a variety of
circumstances. A trooper's day may lead from investigating a fatal
traffic crash to recovering a stolen automobile or apprehending flee-
ing holdup suspects. In approximately half the states, the trooper
with full police powers may be called upon to handle any crime-
related complaint that arises in the unincorporated communities
being served. Then, too, at the request of either municipal officials
or the governor, the state officer may be called into the incorporated
city to reinforce or otherwise aid the local police.

In some state agencies, significant increases in personnel have
been authorized to meet the greater patrol responsibilities on new
expressways and interstate highways as well as the increase in driver
populations, including new-vehicle drivers. Calls to assist local and
suburban police, particularly with specialized functions, including crowd control, also continue to increase.

Salaries for state law enforcement officers are likely, for the most
part, to be fairly comparable to those of police counterparts in the
region served. Beginning salaries are mostly in the $29,000 to
$33,000 range. Some higher maximum salaries for troopers are
found in New York, Alaska, and California, all of which reach
around $42,000. The highest, at this writing, would appear to be
New Jersey in the upper $40,000 range. Other states where max-
imum salaries are quite attractive by comparison are Texas, Penn-

sylvania, Illinois, and Michigan. Salaries, of course, do not include benefits and other compensations such as the value of a take-home vehicle, overtime, and private employment authorized by the department for off-duty work.

Civilian Positions

In addition to uniformed officers, there are numerous civilians employed by the state. Almost one-third of the total employees of state police agencies are, in fact, civilians. These include technical personnel in state crime laboratories and employees responsible for motor vehicle registration, driver and licensing examinations, and motor vehicle inspection. A person interested in such employment should contact the headquarters unit in the state capital for detailed information and specific requirements and forms.

Consider the personnel required to operate the computers and specialized information systems to meet the legal requirements associated with auto registrations, licensing, and recording and analyzing accident and criminal history information. Writers, photographers, record analysts, statisticians, and technicians of various kinds are needed in many different departments. Crime laboratories will be discussed later in this book. An emerging initiative, designed to impact positively upon community-based corrections, is that of the restorative justice specialist. This new position does community/agency planning for restorative justice projects, which focus on the "restoration of offenders," as in rehabilitation, restitution, victim advocacy, or youthful reintegration into the community. In Minnesota, California, Virginia, Illinois, and Colorado, to name a few, there are now restorative justice planners in the systems already and more such positions are to be expected. Their job titles may be restorative justice planner or even restorative victim coordinator. In Philadelphia they created the first stress manager position to examine departmental policies and procedures to make them less stressful.

Other Regulatory Agencies

Enforcement duties at the state level are by no means restricted to the state police or the highway patrol. A number of regulatory, licensing, and protective functions exist that also require competent personnel. Examples of these many agencies are included in the list of California agencies that follows.

This list was chosen because it is perhaps the most inclusive insofar as state responsibility for licensing and regulation goes. All states have these various functions performed in some manner, but they may not be accomplished through specific departments and agencies. A person interested in a career that includes enforcement responsibilities but has as its main mission something other than traditional policing would be well advised to consider some of these employment opportunities. For instance, someone particularly interested in outdoor activities and nature might consider a career in a state regulatory agency that protects wildlife or preserves our natural surroundings. Certain state agencies exercise limited policing functions in such widely diversified fields as communications, public health, transportation, and welfare.

Governmental Units Possessing Police Power in the State of California

Department of Agriculture
Division of Dairy Industry
Division of Compliance
Division of Plant Industry

Division of Animal Industry
Department of Alcoholic Beverage Control
Department of Corrections
Department of Youth Authority
California Disaster Office
Law Enforcement Division
Department of California Highway Patrol
Department of Education
Division of Departmental Administration
California Program for Peace Officers' Training
Department of Employment
Division of Public Employment
Department of Finance
Building and Grounds Division
California State Police
Department of Industrial Relations
Division of Housing
Division of Industrial Welfare
Division of Industrial Safety
Division of Labor Law Enforcement
Fair Employment Practice Commission
Department of Insurance
Compliance and Legal Division
Department of Investments
Division of Corporations
Division of Real Estate
Division of Savings and Loans
Department of Justice
Division of Criminal Law and Enforcement
Department of Mental Hygiene

Department of Motor Vehicles
Division of Registration
Division of Drivers' Licenses
Division of Field Office Operation
Department of Professional and Vocational Standards
Division of Investigation
Department of Public Health
Resources Agency
Department of Parks and Recreation
Division of Beaches and Parks
Department of Conservation
Department of Fish and Game
San Francisco Port Authority
Harbor Police
Department of Social Work
State Fire Marshal
Office of Consumer Counsel
Board of Equalization
Department of Business Taxes
State Board of Osteopathic Examiners
California Horse Racing Board
Bureau of Investigations
License Bureau

Of course, it's entirely possible that not all of the above agencies operate in your state; however, it is quite probable that someone performs the functions of these agencies. A wise course of action would be to visit or write the office of the governor or a state administrator, such as the secretary of state or the office of state attorney general. Also, other possible sources of guidance and assistance might be the state's Criminal Justice Standards and Training Commission or Board in the capital city. Of course, most state governments now operate a centralized human resources office to handle statewide employment, and you can always check state websites.

Thus, employment options at the state level are not at all limited. Whether the assignment be park ranger in recreational areas or at historical monuments or inspector for pollution, health hazards, communicable diseases, hazardous environments, fire prevention, wildlife protection, the regulation of dairy and livestock, insurance fraud, industrial safety, banking examinations, or gambling security, one thing remains quite clear: There is job diversity. Newly formed state agencies now exist to deal with crimes and abuses against the elderly and for formal assistance to crime victims. Because of the wide variation of the above listed duties and the differences in their scope and responsibilities, it would be difficult to assign a projected salary, but a reasonable expectation might be in the mid- to high $30,000 range for those with specialized training.

You should keep in mind that most state police and highway patrol headquarters and governmental agencies will operate a website with information about employment and how to apply for positions. A simple search using various keywords and your favorite search engine will help you locate a specific site. Another employment strategy would be to make direct contact with your area/regional office, often called a "troop," and obtain from them how one goes about reaching the Human Resources Office.

4

MILITARY AND FEDERAL SERVICES

THUS FAR WE have examined law enforcement jobs at the city, county, and state levels. We now broaden our scope to include jobs at the federal level and in the military.

The Military

Some very good job opportunities exist in the military services, and it is not unusual to find civilian police personnel who attribute their initial interest in law enforcement to experience gained while serving in the military police, air police, shore patrol, or a military investigative unit.

The Uniform Code of Military Justice is enforced by the military police, and no one should overlook the opportunity to gain this experience. There are ample opportunities for study at specialized schools, for patrol and investigative work, for promotion through the military ranks, and for worldwide assignments, and entrance can be accomplished well before the age of twenty-one.

The military offers valuable training and the opportunity to learn much about law enforcement, and it often helps interested individuals decide about a career in the field. Some use the military experience as their departure point into civilian policing; others remain for an entire career with the military. The military police are found wherever troops are stationed, and their duties very much resemble those of local-level law officers. They operate on military bases, patrol areas where military are located, and are generally limited in their jurisdiction to military personnel or persons involved in illegal activities directed toward military personnel.

In addition to the military police (M.P.s), the Department of the Navy has opportunities in its Naval Investigative Service. Likewise, the U.S. Air Force has its Security Police, primarily in uniform with duties similar to those of the military police. There is also an investigative branch termed Office of Special Investigations.

Let's take a brief look at one of these units. The Naval Investigative Service is largely civilian and has some twelve hundred special agents worldwide. It is responsible for conducting criminal investigations and counterintelligence operations for both the Navy and the Marine Corps. Its broad spectrum of investigation includes sting operations, undercover drug cases, counterintelligence, dignitary protection, antiterrorism, and the investigation of contracting and procurement frauds. The Army's Criminal Investigation Division and the Air Force's Office of Special Investigations are similar in responsibilities.

Requirements for all these special agents are similar in terms of college background, careful screening, and sophisticated training in multifaceted subjects.

Since one may join the armed services well ahead of the age when many local or federal organizations will hire, there are some important reasons, in terms of experience and training, for considering the military veteran. Wise police administrators and government bureau chiefs welcome candidates with military experience because such applicants have already attained a sense of maturity and responsibility, as well as solid training and discipline. In the modern military, one can seek answers to questions without finalizing any enlistment plans. There is a pride among those who gain assignment to the military law enforcement units, and it shows in their bearing, their dress, their attitudes, and their self-confidence.

Federal Agencies

All federal agencies have specific violation categories in which their jurisdiction lies, and this section lists the official responsibilities and duties of each organization. Because of the many diverse opportunities available throughout the federal government, it would be advisable to obtain detailed qualifications directly from the unit in which one is interested. We have included addresses at the end of this chapter to make it easier to obtain career brochures. Many federal agencies exert considerable effort on recruitment and respond well to job inquiries. They can often be found at college career days. And remember: Don't overlook the likelihood of a website for the organization toward which you are most inclined. Your local reference librarian can always help, too, because all of these publicly funded agencies of government have identities that can be reached locally, regionally, or at the national headquarters, and they will list addresses, fax numbers, websites, and other means of communicating.

Most, but not all, federal agencies require a bachelor's degree for entrance, and all expect it of those who aspire to promotion. Some federal agencies are more investigative than enforcement oriented and, therefore, may demand a variety of skills, such as legal training or tax knowledge. The Drug Enforcement Administration needs persons trained in pharmacy, while the border patrol seeks persons who speak Spanish fluently. Also, many federal officers find that they spend a great deal of time on a particular case or series of cases. Customs agents might spend a long time investigating a shipboard smuggling incident; the Internal Revenue Service agent with accounting skills often devotes many hours to verifying failures to pay proper taxes; the Secret Service cannot for one moment relax its watchful protection of the president and vice president; and the FBI agent may need months to solve a violation involving our national security or a terrorist threat.

Because their numbers are comparatively small (approximately ninety thousand distributed among nearly sixty agencies) and their salaries and prestige levels relatively great, federal agents possess high personal qualifications and must survive intensive background investigations. Of the large numbers of applicants for federal work, only the very best qualified are selected. All federal officers must be patient, determined, capable of working long hours, willing to travel on a moment's notice, and independent enough to work alone for prolonged periods. Travel outside of the United States is required in certain departments, and unlike local police officers, the federal agent may devote lengthy periods of time to only a few specialized investigations and make few arrests. The federal role also entails detailed reports and court appearances. Federal agents must be articulate, able to deal with all levels of society, and must always perform as symbolic representatives of American justice.

Since 1983 the federal government has covered all employees under social security. A twenty-year or twenty-five-year retirement in most federal agencies, with pension dependent upon salary attained, makes early departure from government service possible. Many take advantage of this retirement program, thereby creating continual vacancies in federal units. In recent years, increasing requests for more federal assistance have increased the budgets of these organizations. As the population expands, the demand for aid increases, and criminal mobility continues, it can be safely predicted that the United States government will continue to require large numbers of well-qualified and dedicated people to fill these important law enforcement positions.

Table 4.1 lists the largest federal agencies. The official description and specific duties of each federal agency appear in the *Organization Manual.* Educational requirements for most federal agencies include a bachelor's degree. A discussion of salary, taken from the current GS scale, appears in Chapter 5. Most law enforcement jobs are at the GS-7, GS-9, or GS-10 entrance level. Many start at GS-7 and are promoted to GS-9 in the first year, after training. The U.S. Office of Personnel Management operates a website with detailed salary information.

There is no particular magic to entering federal service. The applicant must apply directly to the agency (see addresses later in this chapter). Upon submission of the required application, successful completion of the Federal Service Entrance Examination is required. Certain agencies may require tests for memory and retention in addition to the general federal entrance exam. All agencies will require medical data, physical exams including agility tests, character and background investigations, and exhaustive reference checks. One can expect a thorough review of one's personal history, life experiences, habits, and acquaintances. You can also expect a polygraph exam and interviews of your family, neighbors, and friends. All federal enforcement agencies have their own basic training programs, which can last up to six months. These are designed to equip the new agent with skills needed in the field. Much of the course content relates to federal statutes and various investigative procedures and how to record and report the required events.

Table 4.1 Federal Agencies Employing 500 or More Full-Time Officers with Authority to Carry Firearms and Make Arrests, June 2000

Agency	Full-time employees	
	Officers with arrest and firearm authority	Support personnel
Immigration and Naturalization Service	17,654	11,377
Federal Bureau of Prisons	13,557	18,364
Federal Bureau of Investigation	11,523	16,230
U.S. Customs Service	10,522	8,210
Drug Enforcement Administration	4,161	4,052
U.S. Secret Service	4,039	1,274
Administrative Office of the U.S. Courts[a]	3,599	—
U.S. Postal Inspection Service	3,412	811
U.S. Marshals Service	2,735	1,492
Internal Revenue Service, Criminal Investigation Division	2,726	950
National Park Service[b]	2,188	843
Bureau of Alcohol, Tobacco and Firearms	1,967	2,545
U.S. Capitol Police	1,199	164
U.S. Fish and Wildlife Service, Division of Law Enforcement	888	142
General Services Administration, Federal Protective Service	803	412
Bureau of Diplomatic Security, Diplomatic Security Service	617	338
USDA Forest Service, Law Enforcement & Investigations	586	610

Note: Table excludes employees based in U.S. territories of foreign countries.
—Data were not provided by the agency.
[a]Includes all Federal probation officers employed in Federal judicial districts that allow officers to carry firearms.
[b]National Park Service total includes 1,544 Park Rangers commissioned as law enforcement officers and 644 U.S. Park Police officers.

Department of Justice, Bureau of Justice Statistics. Federal Law Enforcement Officers, 2000.

An important feature of federal enforcement is the continuing in-service training officers and agents receive. This is practiced most regularly and effectively at the federal level, although it is desirable throughout law enforcement. Since most agencies have divided the country into field service offices, the prospective federal agent must also recognize that travel is a necessary part of the job. On the other hand, as mentioned earlier, one attraction to federal service is the twenty-year to twenty-five-year retirement plan, with a lifelong pension at the appropriate age (fifty to fifty-five) amounting to a percentage of one's highest salary. This plan enables federal employees to complete their careers while still relatively young, then pursue different employment. A number of college criminal justice professors and local police chiefs are retired from the federal services. Likewise, private security, which is discussed in Chapter 7, attracts many retired federal officers. It is important to begin the application process early, whether you are in college or the military, because obtaining a federal enforcement position can take a very long time.

Typical Assignments

Let us review the particular assignments one could expect to have at each of the major federal investigative departments, citing only those duties that are truly enforcement oriented. We will not discuss the many other jobs in those departments that have to do with planning, communications, training, equipment maintenance, records, data analysis, as well as information distribution, inspection or regulatory duties, or the constant updating through in-service training.

The positions described in this chapter all require an ability to recognize and develop evidence for presentation to U.S. attorneys, to meet and confer with persons engaged in many kinds of activities, to testify effectively in a court of law, to prepare detailed written reports, to operate a motor vehicle, to be proficient in the use of firearms and self-defense, and to exercise continual good judgment, resourcefulness, and initiative.

The *U.S. Postal Service*, formerly the Post Office Department, was established independently in 1970. Postal inspectors investigate losses and thefts of the mail or property owned by the post office. In addition, investigators and security force personnel protect postal buildings and installations. There are thirty-five hundred officers employed by the Postal Service, most of whom are classified as criminal investigators; others provide security for the Postal Service and all its facilities and assets.

Several major agencies, employing a total of perhaps twenty-five thousand criminal investigators, operate within the United States Department of Justice. Probably best known is the *Federal Bureau of Investigation*, and agents of this unit are responsible for the enforcement of an extensive variety of statutes. The FBI agent may be assigned to national security matters, rights violations, interstate transportation offenses, and the security of both property and personnel of the federal government. Also within the jurisdiction of the FBI are numerous federal acts that pertain to specific offenses, such as bank robbery, kidnapping, extortion, civil rights violations, and espionage. In recent years, the FBI has been given jurisdiction over hate crimes, incidents involving potential terrorists, and other international threats to our national well-being.

The *Immigration and Naturalization Service*, another part of the Department of Justice and one of the largest federal agencies, administers our nation's immigration and naturalization laws and is responsible for investigations concerning all types of aliens. Its uniformed agents, referred to as the border patrol, are on continuous duty guarding all U.S. points of entry. They are deployed by horse, bike, and all-terrain vehicles to apprehend smugglers of illegal aliens, identify persons suspected of violating immigration laws, inspect documents, and be watchful for signs of illegal entry into the United States.

The *U.S. Marshals Service* provides a general enforcement service, from witness protection to asset forfeiture programs. These officers tend to have prior enforcement experience and fill varied types of assignments, which are often low-key and not well known by the general public. Recent legislation granted the Marshals Service authority to enter into contracts and collect fees for operating expenses related to security protection and serving civil process orders of the courts. The same legislation enables the Marshals Service to become involved in jail assistance in exchange for the housing of federal prisoners.

The *Drug Enforcement Administration*, previously called the Bureau of Narcotics and Dangerous Drugs, is primarily responsible for enforcing laws concerning all narcotic drugs. It also controls the registration provisions of federal drug laws, combats illicit narcotics traffic, and regulates distribution of dangerous drugs. This unit has critical responsibility for determining the quantities of narcotics permissible in the country for medical purposes. In recent years, a sizable increase in positions has occurred within this federal agency. More than thirty-three hundred DEA agents operate in the United States and in more than forty foreign countries.

About twenty thousand federal criminal investigators are employed within the agencies of the U.S. Department of the Treasury. One of these agencies is the *Customs Service*, which regulates the importation of goods into the country. The Customs Service is especially concerned with smuggling activities that may occur in our ports of entry. This bureau has many responsibilities pertaining to goods being shipped into or out of the United States. Customs agents find their daily duties varying from examining an incoming traveler's luggage to registering the weight of an incoming vessel. The Customs Service enforces some four hundred revenue and navigational laws, rules, and regulations for the federal government; this organization ensures that revenue is paid for incoming goods and prevents prohibited goods from entering or leaving the country. Their priorities include not only the protection of the revenue system, but the health and safety of our citizens.

Also under the Treasury Department is the *Internal Revenue Service*. In general, IRS agents' assignments encompass the U.S. tax revenue system. Agents of this organization, many of whom are professional accountants, perform a variety of duties. They examine taxpayers' records to determine tax liabilities and investigate cases involving tax fraud or evasion of tax payments (such as those pertaining to business or gambling). The IRS employs some thirty-three hundred agents.

Within the Treasury Department are special investigators of the *Alcohol, Tobacco, and Firearms Bureau*. They enforce federal laws governing the manufacture, sale, distribution, and possession of firearms and explosives, alcohol, and tobacco products. Agents of this division regulate and maintain records on the legal taxable production of alcoholic beverages and have authority to apprehend those who are engaged in illegal activities relating to alcoholic beverages. ATF agents direct much of their effort against terrorist groups, organized crime, and anyone involved in bombing incidents. Perhaps best known for their work in illicit distillery investigations, the ATF also is empowered to seize and destroy illegal alcohol production and distribution networks and to reduce the smuggling of contraband cigarettes and other untaxed tobacco products. Some two thousand agents bear the responsibility for investigating criminal usage of firearms and explosives and the nonpayment of taxes on products mentioned above.

The *Secret Service* has a twofold responsibility: protecting the president and vice president of the United States, along with their families, and protecting the coins and securities of the government by enforcing laws pertaining to counterfeiting. With more than thirty-five hundred agents, the Secret Service also protects the White House, the Treasury Building, and its Foreign Missions Branch and foreign embassies.

Some nine hundred federal protective officers are under the control of the *General Services Administration*; they are uniformed and authorized to protect property and life within federally owned and operated buildings and adjacent grounds and parking areas. Vulnerable entry points and the like are all monitored or secured to maintain law and order on government property.

There are eleven hundred men and women employed to police some forty blocks in the heart of the nation's capital and miles of inside corridors. Referred to in Washington guidebooks as "polite and attentive," this group since 1801 has been known as the *U.S. Capitol Police*. Like all other police patrol units, they issue citations, search packages, check violations, and ensure visitor and staff security. They are also responsible for the protection of members of Congress and those who attend committee hearings and all events that occur within and around the Capitol grounds. A large number of federal agencies also employ criminal investigators within their own *Offices of the Inspector General (IG)*. These officers, some twenty-seven hundred in number, investigate violations and prevent and detect fraud, waste, and abuse related to federal programs and operations. IG criminal investigators are located within departments such as defense, treasury, housing, and health and human services.

Should one have an interest in law enforcement and wish to follow up that interest by protecting our environment, one of the newer special agent positions is that with the Criminal Investigation Division of the *Environmental Protection Agency*. These officers work within a structure of sophisticated science and technology to protect our air, water, and land resources. Likewise, the *Department of Energy* employs sworn personnel.

Additional Federal Government Assignments

Within the federal government, there are many other units with enforcement and supervisory responsibilities, such as the Federal Aviation Administration, Occupational Safety and Health Administration, Mining Enforcement and Safety Administration, Public Health Service, Bureau of Sport Fisheries and Wildlife, and Food and Drug Administration. For example, there are more than seven thousand federal food inspectors, as well as two thousand investigators employed to check on compliance with civil rights statutes. Even less known to the general public, but still offering attractive career opportunities, are such federal positions as the one thousand Office of Federal Investigations staff working from the Office of Personnel Management (OPM), who conduct personal and record inquiries into backgrounds for federal service applicants, and 150 Consumer Product Safety Commission investigators. In addition, the person who enjoys farm and rural life should not overlook the fact that more than eighty-four hundred investigators work for the Agriculture Department. For those interested in game, wildlife, and outdoor recreation, the Department of the Interior employs nearly twenty-two hundred investigators for its parks and wildlife refuges. In addition, the General Services Administration employs nearly thirty-five hundred persons to conduct criminal and civil investigations of collusion, bribery, conflicts of interest, thefts from government jurisdictions, and offenses specified in the acts protecting government personnel and procedures. The National Park Service, employing more than twenty-two hundred sworn personnel, offers some of the most fascinating and appealing assignments in the federal service. This includes the U.S. Park Police and the Park Service Rangers; both possess authority reaching throughout the National Park system. What an enviable career for those inclined toward biology, wildlife, and the outdoors!

A few others worthy of specific mention, because of their uniqueness and specialization, are the Tennessee Valley Authority (740 officers); the U.S. Forest Service (800); and the U.S. Fish and Wildlife Service, whose refuge officers and special investigative agents total more than 800 personnel. Other federal agents with police powers work for Amtrak, the Diplomatic Security Bureau, the U.S. Mint, and the Bureau of Indian Affairs.

In addition to the large and well-known federal enforcement organizations, there are many independent agencies responsible for highly specialized and technical enforcement. These include the Federal Communications Commission, the Federal Maritime Commission, the Federal Power Commission, the Nuclear Regulatory Commission, the Federal Trade Commission, the Federal Emergency Management Agency, the National Aeronautics & Space Administration, as well as the Interstate Commerce Commission. The latest arrival on the federal scene, and too new to provide much career information about itself yet, is the Office of Homeland Security. Doubtless, as time proceeds, this agency will be responsible for airport, harbor, and port security along with other locations deemed sensitive. The newly revived Sky Marshal program is likely to closely resemble the border patrol, and salaries there begin at $35,000.

Beyond criminal investigative positions in the federal government, there are numerous intelligence specialists whose primary duties relate to background clearances and security personnel matters. These include persons employed by the Central Intelligence Agency, National Security Agency, and Defense Investigative Service, and special agents of the Department of State and Office of Federal Investigations.

One statistic of interest to career aspirants is that although the U.S. government employs its enforcement personnel literally throughout the world, the majority are assigned in California, with the next largest numbers in Texas, New York, District of Columbia, Arizona, and Florida.

For More Information

Those who are interested should contact the following federal agencies directly for specific career information. For the most part, the largest ones all have their own websites, which you can find by typing the agency's name into a search engine.

Department of Defense
Department of Health and Human Services
Department of the Interior
Department of Justice
Department of State
U.S. Coast Guard
Department of the Treasury

Department of Transportation
General Services Administration

The U.S. Office of Personnel Management, formerly known as the U.S. Civil Service Commission, maintains a register or list of qualified candidates for many of the positions described in this chapter. Contact must be made with that office to establish the basic qualifications for any particular position and to obtain the proper application forms and other related materials. Plan well ahead in pursuing federal jobs because turnover is often low, salary and benefits are significant, and there may well be a lag between the time of first inquiry, being placed officially on the qualified list, and finally being hired.

For additional assistance and information, contact the Office of Personnel Management, 1900 E Street, Washington, D.C. 20415, or the Division of Federal Investigations, Personnel Management Office, P.O. Box 7544, Washington, D.C. 20044-7544 or opm.gov.

5

EMPLOYMENT AND COMPENSATION

CRIMINAL AND CIVIL justice is a highly personnel-intensive activity. In recent years, state and local governments have been spending 81 percent of their law enforcement budgets on police salaries. Salaries make up a lower proportion of spending for corrections (59 percent), primarily because of the costs of building and maintaining institutions. Estimates about the cost of crime to government reached $80 billion in 1993 and exceeded $112 billion by 1995. At this writing, it would appear that costs for direct justice services have reached $125 billion. These are actual budget expenditures, not losses, and about half of that amount was spent at the local level of government. Another way of measuring expenditures is to observe that half of every justice dollar is spent for police and law enforcement protective costs; locally, about half of every tax dollar goes to support the local public safety systems. These points have remained constant over the years.

State and Local Salary Ranges

The salary progress that law enforcement has achieved in recent years relates to several factors: the state standardization of training, the awarding of state certification, educational progress toward individual professional stature, and a general increase in public support and community recognition of the duties of police officers. Starting and maximum salaries are both quite competitive with the salaries offered by other employers who seek personnel of the same age, educational level, and personal credentials. The average salary for police officers has increased at least 50 percent in the last decade, and significant numbers of police patrol officers now work in cities where the maximum salary is more than $50,000 and may be even higher with overtime.

Let us review some starting salaries as selected communities reported them in 2000. San Jose, California, advertised for beginning officers at $45,000, with increases going to nearly $55,000 after several years. Historically, California has led the nation in police salaries. One of the best-known departments, the City of Los Angeles, advertises an entry-level salary of $38,000 for a police officer who is twenty-one years of age and has a high school diploma. For successful applicants with college preparation, the salary begins at $42,000. Salaries for Los Angeles patrol officers with experience can reach $62,000. A recent advertisement from the San Francisco Sheriff's Department offers $40,000 for starting deputies with a maximum up to $59,000. One of the nation's premier departments, Berkeley, California, starts its new officers at $57,000, and a maximum officer level can reach $74,200.

It should be noted, too, that cities such as San Jose, California, and Bellevue, Washington, require that their police candidates have higher educational achievements, up to and including a two-year college degree. The Miami-Dade (Florida) County Police Department starts an officer at $35,000 upon academy completion, and the top of their officer salary scale is now reaching $46,000. In Texas, in cities such as Houston and Dallas, there are competitive salaries ($35,000) for candidates. The New York City Police Department reports a starting salary of more than $40,000 as well. The city of Miami now begins its officers at $35,000 with annual increases beyond $40,000. Next door, in Miami Beach, the police starting salary is also $35,000, and the maximum salary is over $40,000. Also in Florida, the cities of Coral Gables, Gainesville, and Tallahassee all require two years of college to enter their police departments. Coral Gables pays $37,000 to start.

In the Midwest, Kettering, Ohio, police begin their officers at $36,000 per year. This agency requires either prior experience or two years of college. Also in the Midwest, Madison, Wisconsin, advertises that it is a police department where young people would want to work. Its ad states that the department is committed to employee involvement, problem solving, and community-oriented policing. It boasts the type of organization where individuals can and do make a difference. Its starting salary is about $38,000.

To illustrate the variations within a rather close geographical region, consider that the capital city of Harrisburg, Pennsylvania, starts officers at $32,000 and nearby Northern York Regional Police starts them at $31,000. In the same area, a Pennsylvania state trooper begins at $30,000. The top of the scale for a trooper is $33,000; in Harrisburg, officers make up to $39,000, and in York Regional, the top scale for an officer is $41,000. Portland, Oregon, advertises $33,000 for entry-level officers and, again, this is with two years of college. In Jackson, Wyoming, the ad lists $32,000 up to $35,000 for basic police patrol officers. In DeKalb County, Georgia, bordering Atlanta, the basic salary is listed at

$32,000. Baltimore, Maryland, advertises at $36,000 and Omaha, Nebraska, in the heartland of America, offers $36,000 with a maximum going up to $46,700. The Denver area offers a top patrol officer salary up to $50,000 after starting in the mid-$30,000s. In nearby Longmont, Colorado, the starting salary reaches $42,000. In Breckenridge, Colorado, the range is $38,000 to $53,000.

As you can see, salaries do vary depending on the type of agency and its size, geographic differences that reflect themselves in regional industrial competition, historical reasons, and how public employment and local government generally have fared in that region over time. And again, be sure to determine if college experience makes a difference in the salary. In many of the agencies listed above, higher education credentials do make that difference.

It is wise to make careful comparisons that reach beyond the basic entrance salary figure. How many pay steps are there before reaching the top of the officer scale? What has been that organization's history with regard to pay increases and increments? What financial reward does promotion bring, and is it significantly higher than the rates paid to the patrol officer rank?

It has been observed for many years now that police officers often enjoy higher salaries than do those workers in other public service careers and other categories of public employment. These other personnel include social workers, nurses, public school teachers, child-care workers, and journalists. Some of these other occupations also require more formal education and specialized training. Furthermore, the evidence continues to mount that policing is a career field on the move upward: income levels have been steadily rising, police officers receive overtime for extra duty, special hazard pay is available for certain assignments, and many locales now award incentive pay for educational and training attainments. Anyone seriously considering employment in law enforcement should seek out those progressive agencies that provide monies for educational attainment and reward earning of degrees.

Some estimate that more than half of all cities offer incentives or salary increases for higher education or specialized training. A decade ago only 37 percent of the departments reported such incentive programs. A 1988 study by the Police Executive Research Forum in Washington, D.C., reported that nearly 14 percent of agencies surveyed required some higher education for police entrance. A typical salary incentive plan, whether state supported or local, may add an additional fifty dollars per month for an associate degree and one hundred dollars per month for the bachelor's degree.

Students are well advised to seek out agencies where incentive pay is available for higher education, not merely for the additional salary it offers, but more importantly because it suggests a commitment to professional stature and top quality that is most important in seeking one's career affiliation. A good rule of thumb, for career guidance, is to look at the basic salary for academy study and immediately upon entrance, the range for entry positions, and what the top-level command jobs pay. Also, see if they provide educational incentives, such as paying college tuition upon successful course completion.

Salary variations are important to anyone seeking a career, and it is always advisable to obtain the latest salary figures from the specific department of interest. This information is easy to obtain and will usually be quoted in any job vacancy notice, even in local newspapers and ads. With contract negotiations occurring in many jurisdictions, and with the general fiscal priorities that police protection enjoys, a salary quoted in print may be out of date by the time the applicant is sworn into the position.

All recruiting notices should outline salary and fringe benefits, as well as required workweek, paid holidays, policy for leaves and sick benefits, life insurance, and so forth. It must be emphasized that because these matters are constantly improving, no figures should be regarded as definitive unless they are from the agency's own official notice. And again, extra pay may be available for hazardous duty with motorcycles, helicopters, patrol boats, or as a dog handler, to say nothing of overtime and court time when you are not scheduled to be on duty. Officers may receive additional percentages for midnight shift duty or for teaching in the academy during off-duty hours. Of course, promotion to higher rank brings additional income. In most jurisdictions, assignment to the detective or investigative unit adds additional salary, perhaps in the form of adjusted anticipated overtime or clothing allowance.

It would be difficult in a national publication to discuss salaries above those at the entry level. It can be assumed that moving up the rank structure brings monetary increases, in addition to the normal pay raises based on seniority. One method of gaining insight into the career potential for remuneration is to look at what the top jobs pay. Again, they vary widely. Some sheriffs who serve as constitutional officers, some state police superintendents who serve as members of the governor's cabinet, and some city chiefs of police earn in the range of $90,000 to $120,000. A recent 2001 advertisement for chief of police in Denton, Texas, listed a salary range from $87,000 to $97,000, with performance-based options raising the salary even higher.

To cite a few illustrations of top-level command salaries, note that the chief of police in Ft. Lauderdale, Florida, earns $81,000 to $124,000. His counterpart in St. Petersburg, Florida, cannot exceed $111,000. Salary for the new chief in Riviera Beach, Florida, is up to $84,000. The chief of police for the city of Laramie, Wyoming, is reportedly paid up to $67,000. In Washington, D.C., the chief's salary is slightly more than $95,000. In suburban Rockville, Maryland, the chief can earn from $83,000 up to $126,000. Cities such as New York, Los Angeles, Chicago, Houston, and Philadelphia, all report paying their police chiefs in the $150,000-plus range. The county of St. Louis, Missouri, offers approximately $90,000 to $124,000.

Clearly, not all careerists can expect to achieve the position of chief of police in their particular locale, and salaries such as commissioner in New York City or chief in Los Angeles may not be typical anywhere else. But there are many high-level officers who enjoy comparatively high salaries. The titles of deputy chief, assistant chief, deputy commissioner, along with lieutenant colonels and majors, all attain salaries only slightly less than that of the top administrator, and these are all realistic goals for the serious, career-minded professional. It is clear in all the above-mentioned chief positions that a college degree, along with considerable managerial experience, is not only required, but also expected. Many cities even list the types of management training and in-service institutes that are expected of the candidate.

Although there may be only one chief, sheriff, or director, there may be a team of half-a-dozen top command personnel supporting policy decisions. These officials, usually the products of that organization, will be paid salaries well within reach of the chief's. Again, to use our illustration of the Miami-Dade Police Department in Florida, the current range for a division chief, of which there are several, is $90,000 to $95,000.

Fringe Benefits

In addition to competitive salaries, enforcement agencies traditionally have offered many fringe benefits comparable to or exceeding those of private industry. For many years, law enforcement has advertised and prided itself on the retirement system it made available to officers. Likewise, sick and injury leave provisions have been attractive. Generally speaking, after twenty years of service, officers can retire with a specific percentage of their highest salary. Most likely, this can be done at age fifty or fifty-five. Should the employee remain with the agency for twenty-five or more years, the percentage of salary paid for retirement increases accordingly. Police officers often retire at age fifty-five, while those in business or industry have another ten years to work before the usual retirement age of sixty-five.

Group health and life insurance programs are universal in law enforcement work. Vacation, holiday, and other leave arrangements are considered routine policies and will not vary greatly among communities. Of course, disability insurance exists in the event an officer is injured in the line of duty.

Local-level law enforcement provides relatively good job security, most likely through a form of civil service or local merit system. Then, too, many more communities now have unions or police employee associations to afford further job protection.

Again, as with salaries and upward mobility, job applicants should ask questions about hospitalization insurance, dental and vision plans, leaves for maternity where applicable, and other benefits. Such an item as overtime provisions can be very important when making salary comparisons. Likewise, off-duty approved employment is often available and encouraged. Some communities have various arrangements to promote and reward higher education. The job seeker is well advised to inquire about tuition payment plans, tuition reimbursements, and any salary incentives for educational attainments.

Typically, most police agencies operated a work schedule that reflected three eight-hour shifts, often rotating personnel every week or two. Drawbacks to the traditional work schedules were many, especially for the small- and mid-sized departments. It has become important that officer strength reflect the workload and the activity levels in the community. At the same time, it is more recognized that officers have family needs and seek more flexibility as in three-day weekends. One accommodation has been ten- or twelve-hour shifts; morale tends to be improved under such circumstances, and many ten- or twelve-hour day departments indicate their productivity has improved. There is more time off for the officers' personal lives, and the department has less downtime for shift changes and between-shifts time losses. Also some agencies change or rotate the working shift infrequently in order to provide officers with more stability in their personal life adjustments.

As unions and collective bargaining units have entered into governmental work, indications are that fringe considerations, working conditions, and specific benefits are now all an important part of employee-employer negotiation and contract.

There are other potential costs and expenses that are important to ascertain prior to deciding upon an agency. In many cases all equipment and uniforms are furnished; in others the officer may have to purchase these. Good career planning requires review of these various factors, since many young recruits are not in a position to make heavy initial monetary outlays in order to obtain a job.

Many people believe that one of the greatest advantages of a police career is the regularity and security of employment, particularly in times of economic instability. This security doubtless has attracted applicants over the years and will continue to do so, especially when coupled with the early retirement age and the resulting pension. Many law enforcement employees, dating back to those who entered law enforcement careers following World War II and the Korean War, had retired and had pursued productive work in second careers. These second careers have ranged from industrial and retail security to college teaching and practicing law.

Like military careers, law enforcement offers the advantage of a lifetime pension while one is young enough to engage in further vocational interests; yet as in the military, many individuals remain in law enforcement because promotions have created new opportunities. Or one may move to another organization and serve in a civilian capacity or become chief executive in a new location entirely. Whatever your choice, opportunities continue to surface as one obtains more experience and expertise. Some of the newest positions that have been created have been filled by those who retired from law enforcement at an early enough age to continue in the productive workforce.

In either case, the retirement fund is a forced savings account at an attractive interest rate, and it is usually more than matched by the employer. This fund also ensures an income in case of early retirement because of disability, and it provides family benefits in case of premature death. In addition, the Public Safety Officers' Death Benefits Program, which began as part of the Crime Control Act of 1968, has been increased. The death benefit paid by the federal government is now $146,000. This legislation also adds a cost-of-living adjustment to the benefit amount. This legislation applies to on-duty, work-related deaths and is for both police and correctional officers. In 1999 the Justice Department extended further support by providing higher educational financial assistance to eligible survivors. Although retirement and death benefits may not be an officer's greatest concern, it is important to note that law enforcement compares very favorably to other occupations in that regard.

Other Incentives

One of the strongest attractions of the police service for ambitious individuals is the opportunity to rise through the ranks. Although this opportunity varies considerably, depending on the size of the department and personnel turnover, it is still something that most successful officers seek, because promotion brings higher pay, additional responsibility, and greater prestige. Because most promotions are made from within the organization and almost always occur after the individual has served several years in a particular rank, few outsiders are found in supervisory and command positions. Although enforcement agencies do employ chiefs or commissioners who have not previously served in the organization, the general pattern has been that those at the top have worked their way up through the ranks.

The important qualities in promotion are not unlike those in any leadership role: sensitivity, leadership, good judgment, dependability, self-confidence, ability to delegate authority, persuasiveness, skill in communicating with and motivating others. One of the most important contributions made by higher education in the law enforcement field has been the intellectual improvement of officers so that they are better equipped to succeed in promotional examinations. One must recognize, too, that most enforcement agencies have requirements relating to the number of years that must be served in a particular rank before one is eligible to compete for the next rank. This is not necessarily a serious restriction; requirements have been reduced gradually as training and education became more acceptable in lieu of lengthy experience. Then, too, law enforcement tends to be a young person's occupation, and there is considerable opportunity for upward movement due to early retirements.

Of course, it is virtually impossible to predict a person's chances for reaching a top position—that of a police chief or a sheriff or state police commissioner. Many individuals have achieved these positions with relatively few years in patrol and investigative assignments. Their appointments were based largely upon the leadership and administrative talents they demonstrated in the lower ranks. Top positions, such as sheriff, are generally the direct result of political appointment or election; many persons would prefer to achieve a command position with direct responsibility for the delivery of services, remaining there for the duration of their career.

Federal Salary Ranges

In the federal law enforcement agencies, salaries tend to be higher than in local and state government, especially after one attains several years of experience as well as uncontrollable overtime.

For the most part, anyone seeking employment in the federal career system will become a part of the government service, General Schedule, pay plan. This system provides for annual pay steps, and employees typically advance one step up the GS scale after each year of service. Pay raises are determined by congressional action and in typical years have averaged between 4 and 5 percent. Agencies vary as to entrance level because of the differences in educational qualifications, specific duties, and types of specialization required. Nonetheless, most federal law enforcement officers will be paid within several of the GS categories described in the following examples. There are jurisdictional differences that exist according to location and cost of living.

Let us consider a GS-7 agent who begins employment with the Drug Enforcement Administration or the Bureau of Alcohol, Tobacco, and Firearms. This typical special agent applicant would possess a bachelor's degree and perhaps some graduate study or investigative experience as well. The new GS-7 can expect to earn $32,343 to start and reach $44,500 with overtime on the same schedule. Many federal agents receive overtime pay, and sometimes that can be as much as 25 percent of their base pay. They can assume that they will travel, work extended daytime duty, and be needed on weekends, and that all of that will accrue overtime payments.

The GS-9 federal position generally requires the bachelor's degree plus graduate study, a law degree, or as much as five years of related investigative experience. The GS-9 starts at $37,647. Under the current salary scale, the average agent would be earning a base salary of $53,517 after adding overtime. Top step on the GS-9 scale, achieved after ten years of service, would be over $60,000, using the current schedule.

In terms of career advancement, we might take the example of a GS-11 who headed a district administrative area and had a dozen years of federal service. An estimated salary for that manager would be $70,000. For a careerist even higher in the administrative structure, perhaps a GS-12, with similar seniority, the salary could reach $85,000. Reviewing this further, it is easy to see how a senior supervisor, with overtime and normal pay step progressions, could expect to be earning within the range of $60,000 to $80,000. To repeat, pay raises can be expected to be in the 4 percent range as they have been for recent years. Also, federal government employees are now under the Social Security Act in addition to the attractive federal pension system.

Other federal service job benefits are equally attractive. They include travel, the opportunity for transfer, and one of the better retirement systems available in the employment world, sometimes with provisions for retirement as early as age fifty-five after twenty years of service. In fact, retirement at age fifty-five has become more the rule than the exception with federal agents. Other normal fringes include paid vacation and holidays, low-cost medical and life insurance, sick leave and financial protection for injury in the line of duty, and special federally supported death benefits. Federal service also affords a measure of employment security that is important to many.

Before concluding the salary discussion on service with the United States government, we should note that for those who reach the top of their agency structure, the earnings rise accordingly. A GS-15, for example, receives a step-one base salary of $80,000 and up to $95,000 after ten years service. Deputy administrators, assistant directors, and titles such as those are paid in the range of $100,000. Presidential appointees can earn as much as $160,000.

One variation worth noting is the Federal Bureau of Investigation. That agency begins its special agents at level GS-10, where the salary is $42,000. Hence, a new GS-10 agent, with administratively uncontrollable overtime (25 percent) would be earning more than $50,000. Most FBI agents are in the category of GS-13, which begins at $65,000. Supervisory special agents are started in the GS-14 schedule, at over $75,000.

Planning Your Career

We have now reviewed many of the rewards of a career in law enforcement. Each aspirant must weigh objectives with the many other considerations and think in terms of a career plan. Law enforcement, unlike most other occupations, offers two choices: a steady, long-term commitment with early retirement, or a shorter duration of active duty followed by numerous other endeavors limited only by imagination. Consider the ultimate example: joining a police department or a federal agency at age twenty-one and then retiring after only twenty or twenty-five years.

The concept of a career development plan is receiving widespread attention and some implementation in modern law enforcement organizations. Although not entirely a new idea, the use of such a plan in most criminal justice agencies is rather recent. For many years, the military and most federal departments have offered employees a career development approach that embraced special training, varying assignments, and opportunities to be rewarded and recognized according to individual desire and capability.

In years past, police career development plans were quite informal and individual but resulted in many former law enforcement officers leaving their original agency and moving on to become public safety directors, college professors, heads of private security operations, as well as judges, legislators, and mayors. This mobility factor strongly suggests to the young career aspirant that other alternatives will come his or her way when an entry job is combined with formal education, relevant training, determination to succeed, and willingness to carefully consider new options. Preparing for retirement and a second career is a truly unique feature of working in criminal justice.

Frustrations

Dedicated service to others can be demanding, and police officers are among those who must perform their duties under conditions that are not always comfortable. Nor can such a career be regarded as routine. All jobs, of course, have disadvantages, so in any occupation one can expect to endure some long hours, difficulties in getting ahead, daily frustrations, and disappointments. However, most law enforcement officers must contend with shift rotation, and regardless of experience, it is never psychologically or physiologically easy to start the day's work at midnight. Stress has become a job-related illness that law enforcement administrators and psychologists are trying to prevent and alleviate. Many agencies now offer their employees a training program on nutrition, exercise, and stress-reduction techniques.

Few occupations are as demanding on the emotions or as conflicting to one's logic and sense of reason as police work. Behind many of the daily difficulties of police work is public apathy. Its causes are numerous and hard to understand, but unfortunately all employees of the criminal justice system feel its impact. The public reflects its apathy through limitations of funds, lack of continuous support, indifference to the causes of crime, refusal to cooperate with authorities, and a frequent disinterest or disenchantment in the police as a unit of government and society.

Public apathy is communicated to the police officer through political leaders who fail to stand behind enforcement actions and through a public that demands equal compliance with the law but expects personal immunity. Officers sworn to uphold all laws can lose their personal idealism when they discover that citizens really expect something less of them.

Social alienation and citizen distrust continue to be major officer frustrations and can cause attitudinal changes if officers encounter them too frequently. The continuing efforts to maintain community policing and citizen involvement are strategies designed to counteract this "we/they" syndrome. There are acceptable mechanisms for coping with job and organizational stress, and the wise leadership in any organization makes every effort to reduce the consequences of known stresses.

The Element of Danger

An element of danger always exists in the life of a peace officer, and there is ample evidence that physical attacks on officers have increased in recent years. Dedicated guardians of the peace believe the physical risks are outweighed by the advantages of challenge, excitement, and working under a vast array of circumstances, often outdoors. However, any confrontation with people under stress, whether in a domestic quarrel or at a holdup scene, is a potentially dangerous one that calls for physical and emotional courage. And there are no substitutes for good judgment, intensive training, wearing body armor, and remaining alert at all times, even at the seemingly routine events, such as traffic stops and questioning a suspect. Anyone considering a career in law enforcement must recognize that, as the visible symbol of authority in the community, he or she may become the target of those choosing to react against established order. The risk is ever present, but statistics suggest that considering the many thousands of daily encounters between police and the public, relatively few end in injury or loss of life. Training and determined professional bearing equip the officer to deal with hazardous situations. The fact that many police injuries and deaths occur through traffic crashes, stopping vehicles whose occupants are unknown, and domestic arguments is strong evidence that thorough training and disciplined caution are essential.

The number of law enforcement officers killed in the line of duty tends to remain in a fairly constant state. Looking back to 1986, feloniously slain officers numbered 66, the lowest number since the late 1960s. The figure for 1987 was 74; the number for 1988 was 78. In 1992 that figure dropped to 63 but climbed again in 1993 to 70 officers. In the 2000 edition of the *Uniform Crime Report*, the FBI records that 134 officers were killed in 1999. Of that number, 47 died in automobile crashes, 10 were struck by vehicles, 45 were shot, 7 perished in motorcycle accidents, and 11 died in situations other than shootings. For the first time, in 1999, automobile crashes outnumbered police fatalities in shooting incidents.

Another point of significance is that drug-related arrests now account for increasing police deaths, but the majority are still due to arrest situations and investigating suspicious persons or circumstances.

Unfortunately an equal number of officers do lose their lives due to accidents, including helicopters and notably motorcycles.

Assaults on officers continue to be a severe problem, and police officers must use extreme caution in dealing with an unknown situation. It is important, however, to keep these losses in context and recognize that twenty-four hours of every day, police officers are in contact with every imaginable circumstance in their community.

A police officer must constantly deal with human suffering, but, unlike most citizens, the officer cannot permit personal emotions to take control. The job demands that he or she always maintains self-control, always acts with calm efficiency, and displays confidence and courage—while never appearing to lack compassion. Officers face difficulty and tragedy daily, and no matter how hard they may try, the police are often unable to prevent these situations. This dilemma constitutes the emotional burden of a police officer's work where personal safety is always at stake.

Visible public support for the police varies according to the real level of concern that citizens have for the particular laws being enforced. There exists full public cooperation and support for police actions surrounding the kidnapping of a child or the robbery of an elderly woman; less but increasing amounts for drunken driving arrests; and minimal support for strict enforcement of the laws prohibiting gambling or after-hours alcohol drinking.

6

EDUCATIONAL REQUIREMENTS

NEARLY ALL POLICE agencies require a high school diploma for entrance, and between 20 and 22 percent of police departments have some higher education requirement for employment. Many departments have established a college education as a requirement to take promotional exams.

In a 1990 survey by the Police Executive Research Forum, the average educational level of police officers was found to be two years of college, and there is every indication that this trend began well over a decade ago and is continuing. Given the circumstances in the late 1960s (average officer at the twelfth-grade level), the large number of officers involved, and the amount of time required for social change, the progress is impressive.

Whether they enroll in a local community college, attend a university, or enter policing while still in school, the message is clear. It is wise for students to begin their education as early as possible rather than waiting until their careers have been underway for years. Many have done so, but delaying educational development makes it more difficult for officers to achieve their goals.

High School

Some subjects in the high school curriculum will prove especially useful for a career in public service or law enforcement. They include American government, civics, sociology, psychology, economics, and any other courses that deal with the social and human institutions. Students might also be encouraged to pursue mathematics to develop deductive reasoning powers. Laboratory sciences that teach the importance of observing, recording, and accurately reporting one's results are also helpful. The communications arts, learned through the study of writing, literature, and public speaking, are very important. In high schools where business law or other legal subjects are available, the law enforcement career aspirant would be well advised to study this crucial information. In addition, all police officers find skill in typing and using computers to be most helpful. With the introduction of computers into most agencies, a working knowledge of that subject has almost become crucial. Some high schools now offer criminal justice or law enforcement in their curriculum, and anyone interested in such a career should certainly take these courses. There are now even magnet high schools that provide specialized study of the justice system.

College

A student nearing completion of high school should obtain catalogs from several community colleges or universities offering a criminal justice degree to become familiar with specific entrance requirements. Some of these institutions will demand that potential law enforcement majors demonstrate qualifications beyond simply possessing a high school diploma. It is not generally regarded as desirable for colleges to establish rigid physical requirements for entrance into these specialized programs. However, students should realize that physical, character, and background investigations would be conducted by police agencies before an applicant is employed.

Students also should remember that a college degree in law enforcement does not necessarily guarantee employment as a sworn police officer in the agency of one's choice. For this reason, requirements for admission to college programs vary throughout the country. Some programs in higher education operate very direct placement services and maintain formalized efforts to assist their graduates obtain employment. At this writing, academic courses and degree programs are becoming available online, and future careerists should not overlook the opportunities in distance education. One need not live within commuting distance of a campus anymore to take advantage of college classes. Such strategies as work-based studies, available through employer encouraged or sponsored distance learning, have truly become the medium for many who have not previously been able to attend the traditional college classroom.

Described below is a suggested balanced curriculum for both law enforcement and corrections associate degree students. These curricula represent revisions of those prepared by the author and various advisory committees several years ago under a Kellogg Foundation Grant to the American Association of Community and Junior Colleges. They have been altered slightly to accommodate recent trends within community colleges and the criminal justice career field.

Associate's Degree in Administration of Justice/Criminal Justice

First-Year General Education Courses
English/Technical Report Writing
Psychology
Sociology/Criminology
Government

First-Year Technical, Specialized Courses
Introduction to Law Enforcement/Criminal Justice
Police Organization/Administration/Operations/
    Procedures
Juvenile Justice/Delinquency Prevention/Procedures/
    Control
Criminal Law

Second-Year General Education Courses
Math
Humanities/Social Science
Lab Science

Second-Year Technical, Specialized Courses
Police Supervision
Criminal Investigation
Law of Evidence (Procedure)
Police Community Relations/Human Relations

Introduction to Criminalistics
Internship/Practicum/Field Experience
Seminar: Topics

Typical Additional Specialized Courses
Traffic Administration/Control/Regulation
Administration of Justice (Emphasis on Courts and
    Legal Process)
Narcotics/Drug Abuse/Investigation
Computers and Their Usage
Cultural and Ethnic Diversity

Communications skills should be mastered at the community
college level for those preparing for university-level study. Likewise, a community college student should take advantage of
courses in the social and behavioral sciences to better understand
the problems, stresses, and dilemmas encountered by the justice
system and its representatives.

Bachelor's Degree in Administration of Justice/Criminal Justice

To plan for study at the university level, one should first obtain catalogs from institutions offering specialized programs with the appropriate balance of academic preparation in related fields of study.
Persons with higher education find that opportunities arise as their
careers progress, and it is always wise to obtain some knowledge
base beyond the specialized major. Thus, the law enforcement (criminal justice) major may look to business management, public administration, and computer science for electives or even a minor field of

study. The corrections major would do well to develop counseling and other social work skills. The juvenile justice major might study rehabilitation or education to augment a resourceful career.

Many faculty members strongly believe that a broadly based criminal justice major is excellent preparation for law school, social work, or public administration. If criminalistics, that is, the science of laboratory examinations and analysis or forensic research, is the career goal, then an entirely different undergraduate preparation is called for—one in chemistry, biology, or physics with strong preparation in mathematics and computers. An undergraduate major in the administration of justice should assist the university student in developing knowledge and skills needed by an effective practitioner, regardless of the career path later chosen.

Before selecting a bachelor's program, one should determine that it is going to provide a well-rounded knowledge of the discipline and the specialty desired. This means that the curriculum not only address underlying concepts, theories, and principles, but also present the state of the art in terms of current ethical practice. The program must also prepare the student to address problems and complex issues, to employ proper research skills, and to evaluate, analyze, and synthesize issues that confront the implementation of social justice.

Listed below are suggestions for an upper-division academic experience. This assumes that the university student has transferred from a community college where some specialization has been available and that the fundamentals have already been received. Of course, if the university student enters the senior institution as a freshman, the curriculum would still involve introductory courses, criminal law, investigation, and some of the others mentioned previously. (Areas of study listed here describe the subject and are not necessarily course titles.)

Law Enforcement (Police) Option or Specialization
Administration, Planning, & Management
Economic Offenses/Organized Crime
Industrial & Retail (Private) Security
Theories and Practices in Police Agencies
Strategies for Crime & Delinquency Prevention
Case Studies in Legal Evidence & Court Procedures
Criminalistics & Crime Analysis
Human Behavior in Criminal Justice
Community Policing & Problem Solving
Comparative Justice System

Corrections (Treatment and Rehabilitation)
Administration (Adult & Juvenile)
Community-Based Corrections Programming
Correctional Law
Evaluation & Treatment of Offenders
Counseling & Therapeutic Techniques
Conflict Management/Dispute Resolution

Juvenile Justice
Juvenile Justice Law & Process
Strategies for Crime & Delinquency Prevention
Various courses related to behavior, treatment, &
   administration cited above

In addition to the specialization courses, there are common core courses that reflect information necessary for anyone entering the justice system with a bachelor's degree. These might be described as follows:

Courts and Judicial Process
Crime and Delinquency Prevention
Planning and Resource Analysis
Criminal Justice Research
Comparative Justice Systems
Critical Issues or Topic Seminars
Field Experience/Internships
Criminological Theories
Victimology

Additional upper-division skills, not necessarily obtained solely through criminal justice departments, but clearly relevant to career planning, are:

Research & Evaluation Techniques
Policy Analysis and Public Administration
Information Systems/Computer Sciences
Accounting and Auditing Procedures
Counseling & Treatment Techniques
Ethics and Professional Standards

Criminal justice majors should seriously consider a minor in such departments as sociology, psychology, urban planning, public administration, social work, political science, computer science, or business management and information systems. For the laboratory major, the minors would be more physical sciences and mathematics. Emerging topics of specialization that are justice related can be found in more and more colleges and universities. These might include fire safety and fire science, private security and loss prevention, and traffic and transportation safety; there are also degrees devoted entirely to occupational, home, and recreational safety. There are new concentrations in topics such as court and judicial administration; industrial, retail, and business security and computer security; loss prevention; and risk management. Only a decade ago, few would have anticipated academic courses covering such areas as environmental protection and enforcement; human factors and environmental stresses; loss prevention and control; organizational management; planning for change in criminal justice; alternatives to incarceration; substance abuse, addiction, and crime; dispute resolution; restorative justice; deviance and violence; crime mapping; and victimology. An excellent combination of such programs can be found in some state universities, and a student might consider a major combining the justice and safety fields. Those considering law school might mix justice and safety topics with government and business studies. Before making a final decision, a serious student should obtain catalogs from well-established and well-recognized universities in this field. Seek out their course descriptions and options for combining areas, and then proceed according to what these programs provide in breadth. Depending upon the part of the country that appeals to you, broadly based curricula can be found at many institutions of higher learning.

Many schools offer criminal justice degrees, but by reviewing catalogs and program options from some with comprehensive programs, a student can begin to see the potential for a career. For example, one might want to combine public and private sector courses. Another might wish to combine legal and investigative courses with fire safety and fire protection. Still another student could mix traffic safety with research and analysis, while someone else may want a more traditional law enforcement emphasis but with additional studies in laboratory procedures and crime scene analysis. Review the catalogs and then discuss the possibilities with faculty advisors, family members, and especially with persons currently employed in various aspects and levels of the justice and safety systems.

In every state today there are also graduate degree programs; one can obtain a master's degree (thirty to thirty-six credits) with a concentration in policy, management, planning, research, or correctional administration. Persons with graduate training typically enter teaching, research, mid-level management, and some of the newer occupations involving planning, project direction, some community-based initiatives, and organizational analysis. Doctorates are also available in public administration, criminology, and criminal justice, all of which generally lead to teaching, evaluation, and research.

Cadet Program—A Work-Study Plan

Most law enforcement educational programs do not yet provide work experience as part of the formal educational process. However, some students gain law enforcement experience with local agencies during their college careers through full- or part-time employment as records clerks, typists, or in other civilian positions. Such work experience is rarely assessed and bears little resemblance to the carefully supervised and evaluated internship period associated with other occupational programs.

It is essential that expanded law enforcement work-experience programs be established in the future. The community college can make a significant contribution to such programs because of its proximity to occupational life in the community. Community colleges can help the student get on-the-job experience that makes classroom work realistic and increases motivation. In addition to these advantages to the individual, work programs ensure that the college curriculum is being tested each day in the actual work environment. Through the combined efforts of such organizations as the International Association of Chiefs of Police and the American Association of Community and Junior Colleges, a dramatic increase in work-experience programs in law enforcement is forecast in the years ahead.[1]

The concept of the police cadet is by no means new, and the program now appears to be gaining momentum throughout the nation. The basic purpose of police cadet programs is to facilitate police recruitment by employing youths aged seventeen to twenty who demonstrate superior potential for police careers, but who are below the minimum age requirement. In 1994 a federal initiative, termed the Police Corps, was established. It is a scholarship funded by the U.S. Department of Justice, which supports higher education in some twenty states and then expects forgiveness of the funding by working for four years in a sponsoring law enforcement agency. Check your state to see if it participates. Florida and Maryland are two states that offer an incentive such as sponsored higher education and later police service, which is aimed particularly at enhancing community policing, reducing neighborhood crime, and fostering cooperative arrangements that are focused on seniors, children at risk, and other citizens in need.

In some communities, cadets have been given such titles as "community service officer," "public service aide," or "public safety

---

[1] *Guidelines for Work Experience Programs in the Criminal Justice System*, by Jimmy C. Styles and Denny F. Pace. American Association of Community and Junior Colleges, 1 Dupont Circle NW, Washington, DC 20036.

aide." The concept is to help young people enter related careers early and gain experience while attending college. The medical field and various high technology areas of industry do this regularly, and the process provides for a steady flow of motivated and educated persons into an occupational specialty.

In all locations (large cities and small communities) where cadets work, they attend classes, play on their own teams in the police department league, and look forward to the day they can qualify for appointments as patrol officers. They have the potential, individually and as a group, to make important contributions to the department. The program keeps them involved in police procedures through the critical years between graduation from high school and their twenty-first birthdays. It is vitally important to the future of policing to offer such programs and projects and career incentives so that young people are not lost after high school when they are not of age to become sworn officers.

In all locales, cadets work in accordance with departmental policies and procedures and the provisions of a departmental training program. They are subject to specific assignment and instruction as well as frequent review of their work by supervisors. Trainees participate in a departmental program of instruction in modern police methods and duties and perform a variety of miscellaneous prepatrol duties. They also are responsible for performing routine clerical duties such as typing, filing, and preparing police forms and records; operating a telephone switchboard and recording hourly calls from and relaying instructions to street patrol officers; maintaining records of all arrests and missing persons; and recording change of address for vehicle operators' licenses.

In some cities, cadets or aides may work a full forty-hour week at their departmental jobs. Their work is a form of training; they are learning departmental procedures and are becoming acquainted with key departmental functions. Cadets are rotated among various assignments at six-month intervals in order to become familiar with the many aspects of departmental operations. In addition, cadets may be required to carry six units per semester in criminal justice or related subjects. This training is to be accomplished on their own time before or after regular working hours.

Cadets are required to furnish and wear a uniform that is similar to that worn by the regular departmental officers. The cost of the uniform is borne by the cadet.

At age twenty-one, cadets are eligible to take an examination for advancement to police patrol status. A "promotional" eligible list takes priority over the "open" eligible list regularly used in filling police patrol positions. Thus, all successful cadets should be able to become police patrol officers as soon as they reach the necessary age, and assuming they have remained vigilant in terms of the prevailing entrance standards.

Recruit Training

All newly appointed law enforcement officers receive some form of initial training prior to being assigned to their duties. In general, recruits in the federal, state, and metropolitan jurisdictions are assigned to an organized training program that may last from eight to ten weeks or up to six months. New officers in smaller communities have not always enjoyed equal opportunity to prepare for police service, although most were permitted to enroll in academics operated by the large cities or the state agency. Fortunately, new statewide training courses are being made available to more officers than ever before—in some places through the junior and community college systems and in other places through regionally distributed academy facilities. Since most recruit training is now mandated, these job training opportunities have become available to everyone regardless of agency size or location. The statewide availability of modern police training is perhaps one of the most important progressive steps that have been taken in this country in the past several decades.

As state minimum-standards legislation now exists everywhere, local and state officers must attain whatever job certification is required. Thus, whether training is offered by local departments, in a regional academy, or in a centralized state setting, all states have some form of minimum requirements and a curriculum that must be successfully completed. The content and minimum number of hours of required recruit (basic) training varies around the nation. Some states mandate as few as 280 or 320 class hours, but these are rapidly becoming fewer and fewer. The 1990s emerged with a minimum basic requirement in most states more like 400 hours as a norm. There are states with minimum requirements over 600 hours; these include California, Florida, Pennsylvania, and Connecticut. Keep in mind that these figures are required minimum hours of training and many jurisdictions will exceed their state minimums. This increasing of hours over the last twenty-five years sends the message that professional status for sworn law enforcement officers has arrived in most states.

Beyond requirements for recruit training, new emphasis is being placed upon supervisory development so that those promoted to sergeant will have a thorough knowledge of their jobs. In the middle management ranks, such as lieutenant, it is vital that new instruction be offered because patrol and investigative experiences cannot prepare one sufficiently for command assignments. And officials in the top command positions, regardless of street experience, require training in budgeting, planning, and organizational efficiency. No easy method exists for delivering this necessary knowledge to the various assignments, and so we find that a variety of training courses is available, but not necessarily equally throughout the nation.

Recruit training curricula vary among the local and state agencies, particularly with regard to local ordinances, rules, and regulations; use of departmental equipment; and report forms. However, all such training includes lectures and demonstrations on first responder (emergency medical aid), criminal and traffic investigations, traffic control, patrol procedures, legal terms and criminal laws, courtroom testimony, procedures in handling disputes, search and seizure rules, writing citations, crisis responses, courtesy and safety, cultural diversity, interpersonal skills, and many other subject areas related to police duties. The recruit can also expect to spend considerable time on the firing range, learning the service weapon, shotgun, and other weapons in the agency arsenal, including chemical agents. Likewise, the gymnasium will be used for the fitness program and for learning defensive tactics and search and restraint techniques. Operation of the police vehicle will be taught on the driving range, and this usually includes learning to control the vehicle in difficult situations. The more time that can be dedicated to practical exercises and simulations and being tested by proving one's competencies, the better will be the final graduate of the training academy.

The modern police training environment will include presentations about diverse cultural groups, techniques for resolving disputes, officer survival and safety considerations, victim and witness assistance, discretionary and judgmental weapons usage, conducting field sobriety tests, and computer usage.

There is a great deal to be taught in limited class time, so schedules are strict, complete note taking generally is required, and a disciplined atmosphere may prevail. Some departments are rescheduling their recruit training to give new officers an opportunity for field experience in conjunction with classroom study.[2] In recent years, the number of nonpolice personnel employed by police academies has increased, although most lecturers are law enforcement personnel. Experienced agency personnel bring considerable background to the course they instruct, while holding operating costs to a minimum. Guest lecturers, however, are essential. They come from federal agencies, the courts, and a variety of local agencies with which the police regularly deal.

Local community colleges and universities frequently assist police academies by offering instruction on criminology, delinquency, psychology, report writing, human behavior, interpersonal communications, supervision, computer usage, cultural diversity, and other academic topics relating to police work. The future will continue to see more academic preparation being incorporated into police training and an increase in the opportunity to obtain college credits for studies in the recruit-training program.

Most police training includes some exposure to audiovisual techniques and training films because new officers must have the opportunity to observe as much as possible before facing real-life situations. To that end, they will also be required to demonstrate automobile driving habits, participate in a simulated crime scene

---

[2]*Law Enforcement Training and the Community College*, by Denny F. Pace, James D. Stinchcomb, and Jimmie C. Styles. American Association of Community and Junior Colleges, 1 Dupont Circle NW, Washington, DC 20036.

search, testify in a mock trial, and practice such skills as lifting fingerprints and taking photographs. The grading system varies among departments, but tests occur regularly, and students who do not show promise of success can expect to be dropped from the academy. Their grades and efficiency ratings become a part of their permanent personnel record.

State and federal training programs for recruits are often longer than are those for local agencies. They also usually reflect better facilities and a larger budget for this important purpose. Of course, training is designed to accommodate the needs of the particular organization; thus highway patrol officers will focus greater attention on the motor vehicle code and accident investigation, while federal agents will concentrate on the statutes that will be their ultimate responsibility. All, however, have some aspects in common, such as defensive tactics, using firearms, searching prisoners, handling physical evidence, courtroom demeanor, and preparing accurate reports.

Depending upon the type of agency, recruits also spend many hours studying criminal and constitutional laws, community relations and citizen interaction, handling of disturbances, proper radio procedures, basic investigations, and how to recognize and respond to various emergencies. Today's police recruits are also better informed as to their own needs in terms of mental health and stress reduction and the importance of relaxation, positive outlook, good nutrition, and exercise.

The modern police academy, whatever its duration and setting, emphasizes performance and the ability to demonstrate that tasks are understood and can be accomplished. Competency-based or performance-based training, as they are often termed by military schools, are the methods most likely to prove that a recruit can actually save a life through CPR or other procedure, and not simply answer a question about it on an exam. Demonstrating the technique for stopping a vehicle, searching a building, or removing an assailant's weapon means more than writing about the procedure. Through videotaping field exercises and using simulated situations, especially with firearms and defensive driving, the new recruit obtains a realism previously unknown in the academy classroom.

Some of the topics in recruit training have been mentioned previously, but let us look at what else a modern, well-prepared officer must learn about prior to entering police service:

- the role of environmental protection agencies and how pollution control is enforced
- expectation of law enforcement in terms of ethics and standards of conduct
- mastery of legal terminology as well as statutes and basic laws of arrest
- public speaking, report writing, and nonverbal communications, which are crucial
- sensitivity to various groups—minority, handicapped, elderly, or young—and the many facets of drug abuse, alcoholism, and mental illness
- fire fighting as well as recognizing hazards and risks during routine patrol
- dealing with traffic problems, including drunk drivers, congestion, or crashes
- interviewing and routine preliminary investigative techniques and procedures
- crisis intervention skills and proper approaches to calls for service

- proper use of the firearm, baton, handcuffs, and unarmed defense techniques
- managing conflicts and disturbances that arise in neighborhoods and families; domestic violence
- understanding and dealing with tensions and issues that require resolution; community and problem-solving police strategies
- maintaining an alert and safety-conscious status at all times

Following completion of their formal classroom studies, most enforcement officers are assigned to work under the supervision of an experienced officer who must periodically evaluate the new employee's performance. In addition to a supervisor, the recruit may work with a more experienced partner for a time to receive instruction in specific methods and procedures and to ensure that all efforts are in line with departmental policy. Of course, the effectiveness of such procedures depends upon the personnel involved, but all departments agree on the importance of on-the-job training for recruits.

The probation period generally begins upon entrance into the recruit training program. It may continue for at least one year; in some agencies it lasts for two years. During that period, the new officer receives not only classroom instruction, but also field training and supervised on-the-job experience. This transition period is critical to detecting deficiencies in the selection process as well as limitations in the classroom-training program.

After the police recruit has worked under the guidance of the field-training officers, as they are often termed, he or she is eligible for full status as a patrol officer. Performance evaluation continues, as officers must now rely on their own judgment rather than the classroom or an experienced supervisor. Most police administrators strongly believe that observing their performance is the best way to evaluate whether new recruits are suited for a police career. Such views are supported by the fact that the stresses and conflicts of enforcement work cannot adequately be simulated, and, therefore, one must perform duties before being assigned permanent status as a police officer.

In some agencies the probation period is spent rotating from one major division to another to become acquainted with the entire organization. Ideally, performance ratings during the probation period will be frequent, classroom retraining will occur, and conferences with supervisors will be scheduled on a regular basis. In addition, training evaluation from the recruits is becoming increasingly important to the training academy to ensure basic training meets on-the-job needs.

Formal licensing and certification for law enforcement officers occur when they are sworn in to their positions, take the oath of office, and are awarded a badge. As mentioned previously, the state then certifies them as adequately trained and authorized to serve. In all jurisdictions, the badge is the symbol of legal authority, and with it comes the power of detaining, arrest, and other responsibilities for community safety and security. The uniform and badge also symbolize that one is the visible representative of government and authority, and in a democracy this is an important point to recognize when considering the implications of a career choice.

Career Development and In-Service Training

More officers are also being offered in-service training at an advanced level to ensure up-to-date knowledge and skills. Again, as with recruit training, states are beginning to mandate advanced courses for those who expect to be specialists or to be promoted. Most agencies have encouraged career development study in the past, even when conducted briefly and within the department itself.

The subjects may range from handling the mentally disturbed to recent court decisions, but the purpose is to keep officers current, alert, and informed. One of the most effective methods for giving in-service training to all officers is often termed "roll-call training." This technique, a fifteen-minute daily coverage of the practical aspects of policing, was offered in the Los Angeles Police Department in 1948. The information has been published in book form, and today these manuals are used in other police departments throughout the country.

In 1964 the International Association of Chiefs of Police began publishing *Training Key* twice a month. Available to all members of an agency at low cost, it covers a variety of practical police subjects. Each issue deals with a specific topic, such as searching a suspect, handling the mentally ill, or stopping a vehicle. *Training Key* has proven quite successful across the nation, since few departments could afford the research and production costs necessary to produce similar publications of their own.

There also are many opportunities to participate in specialized training through institutes and short courses. These may be provided by community colleges, universities, federal agencies, or by the local departments themselves. Officers assigned to certain specialties must receive training that equips them to deal more effectively with their own areas of concern. Any specialized operation demands greater competence, and police officers cannot assume that experience alone will provide that knowledge.

Courses that occur most frequently include those aimed at specialists in juvenile, violent crimes, criminal investigation, traffic, and more recently, computer use, narcotics, community relations, and planning. In addition, there are programs for those who have the training responsibilities for their departments. A training calendar is provided monthly through the Association of Chiefs of Police's publication, *Police Chief Magazine*. However, there are several agencies and institutions of higher learning that offer regular, well-established programs varying in length from several weeks to several months.

The National Academy, conducted by the Federal Bureau of Investigation, is perhaps the most noteworthy program conducted by a federal agency. This twelve-week session has been operating since the 1930s, and officers from throughout the fifty states as well as many foreign countries are selected to attend. The National Academy has had a significant percentage of its graduates become top-level administrators in enforcement agencies over the years.

The Northwestern University Center for Public Safety (405 Church Street, Evanston, Illinois 60204) affords a variety of specialized courses for enforcement personnel. The nine-month course is particularly concerned with agency management and police administration. In addition to the long course, there are a number of two- and three-week sessions devoted to various topics such as supervision, accident investigation, and most recently, racial profiling.

The University of North Florida, in Jacksonville, operates the Institute of Police Technology and Management and offers unique courses in resource management, budget planning, use of minicomputers, and other topics related to traffic, radar, enforcement procedures, and record analysis.

The University of Louisville (Louisville, Kentucky) has operated the Southern Police Institute for almost five decades. Originally developed to assist officers throughout the Southeast, it now accepts applicants from agencies throughout the nation. It also provides a variety of two-week programs with a special three-month course for in-service, supervisory, and command personnel. Its original purpose was to provide needed skills and understanding for police in the issues confronting social change. It now embraces courses on homicide investigation, sex crimes, supervision, strategic leadership, internal affairs, the command course, and managing the small agency.

The National Crime Prevention Institute, created in 1971, also operates from the School of Justice Administration at the University of Louisville and offers various courses for persons concerned with crime prevention and security.

Several federal agencies conduct specialized courses for local and state law enforcement officers. These include courses on narcotics investigations, hostage and terrorist tactics, explosives and bombs, and surveillance. Currently many of these are available at the Federal Law Enforcement Training Center in Glynco, Georgia. This is where most federal agents receive their training, and it also offers specialty programs to other jurisdictions. The Glynco center does particularly unique work in high-risk topics such as officer survival, executive protection, driver training and potential crash avoidance, hazardous materials, and computer security. The Glynco programs have pioneered training using simulations, from field investigations to firearms usage.

Throughout this chapter we have considered the great importance of career preparation. Relevant high school electives, selecting an agency with up-to-date training, and seeking out additional in-service study and higher education are most important. The law enforcement community affords personnel numerous opportunities for one-day or one-week training, and the wise employee looks ahead to these and seeks them out. Criminal justice is too broad a field of endeavor and includes too many new directions for anyone to consider stopping education after high school. The local community college or state university must be the next step in order to prepare properly for working with our social justice system. Law enforcement training gives one the organizational setting and the formal authority to take charge of situations and to make decisions that really count.

7

RELATED CAREERS IN CRIMINAL JUSTICE AND PUBLIC SAFETY

MANY CAREER OPPORTUNITIES are available throughout the administration of justice and public safety systems. Although law enforcement is the most visible and the job that most citizens recognize, it is by no means the only vocation concerned with the problems of crime and delinquency. Because the police are instantly identified, and their actions are the most reported and commented about, it is no wonder that people thinking about careers in this area focus upon that sector. The fact remains that many other jobs exist throughout public safety, and this chapter will attempt to describe and assess them as valuable and logical alternatives.

Career goals require some early planning, and such factors as higher education, physical characteristics, personal determination, and often family and teacher advice will play a part in setting those goals. Some of the readers of this book, while thinking about law enforcement generally, will want to seek out further information about related endeavors. The student who is interested and successful in high school chemistry and physics should look at the world of criminalistics as it relates to an interest in solving crime. Likewise, the student interested in political science, logic, and government may prefer a career in criminal law. It is important to think of the justice and safety systems as an interlocking group of enterprises with common goals. The paths individuals choose to help our society to attain those goals may differ, just as many vocational choices exist within the wide field of medical services. There are important choices to be made, and gathering accurate information is the first step.

This section will discuss law enforcement as a profession, with the specialties that affect the justice system directly: criminalistics and the forensic crime laboratory, the broad field of corrections and rehabilitation, and the increasing, fast-changing business of private security, loss reduction, the practice of law, and specialized protection services.

The Practice of Law

The practice of law is perhaps the most obvious pursuit of a related career field. A number of legal officers participate in the justice system, and it is not uncommon for persons working in criminal justice to obtain formal legal training as well. (A good source of information for those interested in a law career is *Opportunities in Law Careers*, published by VGM Career Books.)

Let us quickly review the general career options one has after obtaining a law degree, assuming that work in the justice system is still the goal. State and local prosecution offices number more than eight thousand; these are the agencies engaged in the prosecution of alleged criminal offenders, although some also provide civil legal services to government. At the state level, these include the Office of the Attorney General, states' attorneys, district attorneys, and prosecuting attorneys. The titles of county-level prosecutors vary but include county attorney, corporation counsel, county solicitor, and district attorney to name a few. In contrast, a relatively new law-related agency is the Office of the Public Defender, the smallest of all criminal justice sectors. Like the prosecutor's office, these offices are supported by public funds, and their responsibility derives from the constitutional right to legal counsel.

Three-fourths of all public defender offices are administered by county government and less than one-fourth by state government. The office of public defender is growing, and most public defenders now handle the full range of criminal cases, along with some civil areas. Here again is a fine example of a career that relates to criminal law and offenders but also services the needs of persons who seek legal assistance for housing, consumer welfare, and various domestic matters. Public defenders do not merely represent those charged with crimes.

There are about seventeen thousand courts, which represent the second largest sector of the justice system. Courts are units of the judicial branch of government with authorization, by statute or constitution, to decide controversies and disputed matters of fact brought before them. There are appellate, general, and limited levels of court jurisdiction. All of these employ judges, clerks, and private practice attorneys. Some also have court administrators, another relatively new career, to oversee and supervise the process.

A typical court administrator might be employed under the general direction of the chief judge to manage all administrative functions of that court. These functions would include directing a staff responsible for the processing of traffic, civil, and criminal cases, as well as providing court security and many other nonlegal duties. Many positions exist for court administrators that pay in the $50,000 to $65,000 range, and graduate training in public administration or court/judicial administration is required. Future growth is expected, due to continuing state-level court reorganization and the backlogs in courts, which result in delays and political pressures to alleviate them.

Jobs for bailiffs, court officers, and other nonlegal positions affiliated with court expansion are increasing. Both size and number of courts have grown in recent years, and that growth appears to be continuing. With it will continue the demand for maintaining order and the numerous other tasks of the bailiff and court officers. Other positions, such as law clerks, clerks of the court, legal stenographers, and legal transcribers also serve the court system in a supportive capacity.

Judges, who may serve in any number of different jurisdictional levels, basically listen to testimony, rule on what evidence may be acceptable, and either decide the case or instruct the jury on the law and their options for a decision. Numbers of judicial positions have been on the increase, again due to backlogs and increased criminal trials. There are district courts, juvenile courts, traffic courts, appeals courts, probate courts, municipal courts, and, of course, supreme courts. Nearly all judges now have legal training and extensive courtroom trial experience.

We have described briefly the main actors in the court; other lawyers are employed by government to research and prepare legislation. Staff attorneys serve on most legislative committees at both the state and national levels. The police legal advisor has already been mentioned as a newly established career for those lawyers who wish to remain, or to become affiliated, with a police agency. First serving as the local prosecutor or county attorney launches many political and judicial careers. The lawyer, and more recently, the court administrator, are interwoven into our justice and juvenile systems, and many career opportunities are projected for this area of public service.

Corrections and Rehabilitation

With the public expressing increased concern over violent crime, career criminals, and repeat offenders, sentencing trends in recent years have been toward more institutional confinement for longer periods of time. This has resulted in a virtual explosion of the inmate population in federal, state, and local correctional facilities, along with numerous employment opportunities. In fact, if current trends persist, corrections will continue to be the growth industry of the criminal justice system well into the twenty-first century. Distribution of corrections employment shows that 63 percent of correctional employees work for state government, 33 percent at the local level, and 4 percent at the federal level. With prisons alone, there are some 1,419 institutions that house long-term offenders. Juvenile jails and facilities add to this number. Consider that more than 6.3 million people were under correctional supervision in the United States in the latest count. Nearly four million of these adults were under community supervision (probation) and an additional 720,000 were on parole—conditional, supervised release after serving a prison term. This figure represents over 3 percent of the entire U.S. adult population. Each year between 1990 and 1999 averaged a 4.2 percent growth of individuals under correctional supervision.

States with the largest prison populations are Texas, California, and New York; along with Florida and the Federal Bureau of Prisons, they account for 40 percent of all inmates.

With 1.8 million offenders behind bars, the search for correctional officer personnel will continue at a rapid pace for some time to come, and career seekers will do well to give consideration to employment in this important human service occupation. This has been described in national media sources as a "growth industry" since 1985, and it still is. Under community-based correctional services, the objectives of enforcing court orders, meeting client needs, and reducing recidivism may all come together as the future unfolds, under the umbrella of restorative justice enhancing our public safety mission.

Yet, because corrections does not have as much public visibility as do the police or the courts, the wide array of jobs available is often overlooked. Depending upon one's interests, employment in corrections can be found in any number of settings: in an institutional facility as a sworn correctional officer; with a probation office supervising offenders in the community; as a caseworker whose clients require specialized attention; or as a correctional counselor dealing with the personal problems and individual circumstances of inmates, probationers, or parolees. Since institutions—from local county jails to large maximum security penitentiaries—are all communities within themselves, corrections also includes positions ranging from work supervisors to teachers, chaplains, medical personnel, psychologists, and many others, as well as the command staff, most of whom began as sworn correctional officers.

As with police departments, correctional institutions are found at all levels of government. At the local level, one might seek employment in the jail, a stockade, a women's facility, a halfway house, a regional center for youthful offenders, an assessment center detaining juveniles temporarily, or a specialized facility, such as group homes dealing with addictions. Some local jail staffs are employed as deputy sheriffs and are cross-trained in law enforcement to serve as patrol deputies as well.

As reported in the 1998 *Sourcebook of Criminal Justice Statistics*, there were 600,000 persons employed in local, state, and federal correctional facilities as officers. The largest single group of employees in this system is correctional officers. Some 350,000 of the above number work in state and federal facilities. Like their police counterparts, correctional officers are sworn employees at the entry level of the system. Those wishing to advance to higher ranks can always expect to serve for some time as a correctional officer, since most promotions are made from within the agency.

Generally speaking, the correctional officer of today has some higher education, plus training in subjects ranging from emergency response to interpersonal communications. Especially in the case of facilities that specialize in housing and treating youthful offenders, officers may receive special training in modifying behavior.

Illustrative Examples of Work

Specific duties of correctional officers vary somewhat, depending on the type and size of the facility. In smaller institutions, officers are expected to perform a wide variety of tasks, whereas those in more specialized or larger systems may be assigned to one particular duty post. General functions include responsibility for security of the institution, control of contraband (prohibited items), and supervision of the many repair, maintenance, manufacturing, and other inmate work services—from furniture factories to farming operations. In addition, significant counseling functions may be included at those institutions that are committed to the use of correctional officers in the rehabilitation process. More specific tasks include:

- communicating with the inmates to develop effective interpersonal relations and assist their adjustment to incarceration
- maintaining inmate order and discipline by patrolling corridors, inspecting cell blocks, and enforcing rules and regulations
- preventing escapes through visual alertness, promptly responding to any information obtained about escape attempts, conducting routine search procedures, being alert for signs of suicidal behavior
- keeping accurate inmate records upon intake, during confinement, and upon release
- supervising recreation, work details, visiting, and all other inmate activities
- handling inmate problems and requests for services (commissary items, medical treatment, and religious services)
- transporting inmates to court appearances, medical offices, and other correctional facilities
- conducting frisk, strip, and cell searches to detect contraband
- screening visitors to ensure that they are authorized and not introducing contraband
- conducting regular head counts of the inmate population
- preparing written incident reports of rule violations

- providing first aid in emergency situations
- handling any physical altercations with the minimum force necessary to control the situation
- classifying inmates according to their personal characteristics and offense record to make proper cell assignments

In addition to the primary responsibility of keeping offenders safely in custody, the correctional officer in recent years has come to be recognized as an important component of the rehabilitative process. With the limited availability of formal treatment services, and in view of the close and continual contact between staff and inmates, the role of the correctional officer in promoting behavior change is evident. In recognition of this "cell block counseling" role, many agencies are providing officers with additional training in problem solving, human behavior, cultural diversity, and interpersonal communication. After all, the ultimate goal is to prepare that inmate for eventual release and adjustment back into society.

Places of Employment

Numerous employment opportunities exist at both the federal and state and local levels for interested individuals.

Federal Level

Federal detention centers confine aliens detained for the U.S. Immigration and Naturalization Service. The Federal Bureau of Prisons employs approximately twenty-four thousand staff members in facilities throughout the country. About half of these positions are direct correctional services (primarily correctional officers and treatment personnel), but opportunities also exist in related classifications such as educational programs, recreational activities, religious services, food preparation, correctional industries, mechanical maintenance, psychological and medical services, management, and administration. Working for the Federal Bureau of Prisons is working for the federal government and as part of the U.S. Department of Justice. More than two hundred separate occupational categories are encompassed within these seventy institutions nationwide.

Ever since its creation in 1930, the Federal Bureau of Prisons has been a leader in developing modern approaches to correctional planning and management. Its staff is well trained and committed to upholding very high standards of performance. Its operations encompass six regional offices to expedite administration. Career opportunities are available through these six regional offices and through the headquarters in Washington, D.C.

The largest numbers of entry-level openings in the Federal Bureau of Prisons are for correctional officers and treatment specialists. Correctional officers at the federal level perform generally the same functions as their state and local counterparts. They are responsible for guiding inmate conduct, supervising work details, carrying out plans for inmate treatment, instructing and counseling inmates, and ensuring the custody, safety, and well-being of the inmate population. Applicants must be U.S. citizens, no more than thirty-seven years of age, in good physical condition, and subject to a security clearance. Also, applicants must demonstrate that they have had three years of relevant work experience, although completion of a four-year degree may be substituted for three years of experience. Those selected are appointed at the GS-5 level with potential for advancement to the next grade after six months of satisfactory service. Treatment specialists with a degree begin at the GS-6 level and, as with police, overtime is to be expected.

Correctional treatment specialists employed by the Federal Bureau of Prisons perform correctional casework in an institutional setting. They develop, evaluate, and analyze program needs of the inmates; assess their progress; coordinate inmate training programs; develop social histories; provide case reports to the U.S. Parole Commission; develop parole and release plans; conduct individual and group interviews; and coordinate with family members. Applicants must meet the same general requirements listed above for the position of correctional officer. In addition, candidates must have a bachelor's degree with at least twenty-four semester hours of social sciences, plus two years of graduate study in social science, two years of supervised casework experience, or a combination of both.

Regardless of their specific job classification, employees of the Federal Bureau of Prisons are first and foremost correctional workers, with specialization secondary to that primary role. Therefore, all employees participate in a core training program consisting of interpersonal communication skills, firearms, self-defense, hostage policy, report writing, legal issues, employee conduct, supervisory skills, and other fundamental topics. Refresher and specialized training are provided as needed throughout the employee's career.

As with other law enforcement and correctional agencies, the Federal Bureau of Prisons maintains high standards of personal conduct for employees, both in the workplace and in the community. This is perhaps an even greater concern in corrections, where employees work daily with a sophisticated inmate population, many of whom actively seek to manipulate staff. Personal integrity, honesty, and good moral character are therefore essential qualifications of all correctional employees.

The Immigration and Naturalization Service, also within the U.S. Department of Justice, employs eleven hundred detention and deportation officers. Their duties are specific to alien and immigrant matters whenever a federal crime is involved. In recent years their numbers have been increasing since illegal entry and forced deportation of criminal, nonviolent offenders has been getting much public and political attention.

Another group of federal officers, some four thousand in number, is primarily responsible for probation and parole supervision of federal offenders. These officers work for the Administrative Office of the U.S. Courts. Like probation officers, federal pretrial service officers, numbering some six hundred, have responsibilities for investigation and supervision of defendants released to their custody. They are almost entirely assigned to Texas, California, Florida, New York, and other heavily populated regions. A similar distribution would hold true for the detention and deportation officers cited above.

Benefits and job security are some attractive features of federal employment, along with promotional opportunities. However, employees seeking promotion must generally be willing to transfer to other areas of the country. Those covered by the special retirement provisions for law enforcement and correctional personnel may retire at age fifty with twenty years of service, with retirement at age fifty-five available for those with twenty-five years of such service.

Those interested in employment with the Federal Bureau of Prisons can obtain an application by contacting the National Recruitment Office, 320 First Street NW, HOLC Building, Washington, D.C. 20534.

State and Local Levels

The state level offers the greatest number of correctional employment opportunities. More than three hundred thousand employees work in corrections at the state level, which represents 61 percent of the total correctional positions available in the country. Such personnel are predominately employed in the approximately fourteen hundred state adult confinement institutions and the community-based facilities spread throughout the United States. These might include prisons, diagnostic and reception centers, drug or alcoholic treatment centers, prison farms, road camps, boot camps, and community-based settings such as halfway houses, prerelease facilities, and youthful offender institutions. Some 95 percent of inmates housed in state corrections systems are confined in prisons; only about 5 percent are within community-based settings. Employment potential in community-based correctional work varies; some states have no such program, and several states, notably Florida, Michigan, and Pennsylvania, have many. All states have at least one major maximum prison, and highly populated states can have a half-dozen or more.

Listed among the eleven hundred publicly operated juvenile facilities are detention centers, group homes, ranches, forestry camps, and training schools. Many are state-operated, but an equal number are county-administered. Very few are at the city level, although juvenile programs and facilities are increasingly operated by private enterprise. The largest numbers of specialized facilities for juveniles and youth are found in California, with New York and Ohio following. There has been a recent trend to increase the number of smaller, minimum-security facilities in order to focus more specialized treatment and attention on persons with the best hope for rehabilitation. Juveniles with more frequent and serious arrest records were previously housed in local jails. However, courts are now requiring that juveniles be separated from adults, thus creating more separate juvenile facilities, even for the hard-core offender. Although those under eighteen are generally considered juveniles, this varies depending on the jurisdiction, the offender's prior record, and the seriousness of the offense. Overall employment potential is expected to continue to expand for those interested in working with youth, whether in security or various treatment-related positions.

Among institutions housing adults, the nation's 3,365 local jails confine those waiting for trial or sentenced to a year or less, whereas state facilities house those serving sentences longer than one year. In fact, almost half of jail residents are not convicted—meaning that they have either not yet gone to trial or have not yet been arraigned. Jails also hold those awaiting either sentencing or transfer to state prison. As a result, clients in the local system tend to turn over rapidly, and, therefore, less emphasis is usually placed on long-term treatment or rehabilitation. It is also interesting to note that over 30 percent of all jail inmates nationwide are confined in only 5 percent of the jails—those jails holding two thousand or more inmates. For example, the Los Angeles mega-jail system is the largest in the free world, housing a daily population that exceeds twenty-two thousand inmates. With thousands of staff members servicing the security and general living needs of inmates in mega-jail systems, it is apparent that better employment and promotional opportunities will be found among the larger jails in major metropolitan areas. However, opportunities are expanding in many smaller jurisdictions as well, and the two hundred thousand personnel working in local corrections and detention represent 35 percent of the employment in corrections nationwide.

Since jails are the first point of contact for offenders, they are also the first to feel the impact of increasing crime rates. To reduce jail populations to more manageable levels, pretrial release programs and electronic monitoring are being used more often as an alternative to incarceration. These efforts involve selecting offenders whose community ties, work record, and lack of prior convictions make them good risks for appearing at trial. Many are released into the community with close supervision. Others are placed in home detention through the use of electronic surveillance that monitors their movements outside of a specified area. These new trends toward home detention and pretrial release have created additional jobs for correctional personnel supervising the activities and reporting requirements of those released. Some pretrial release programs fall under the jurisdiction of the courts; others are the responsibility of the local jail system.

Administratively, the majority of jails are managed by a sheriff's office or a separate city or county agency, and some jails are even administered at the state level. These include Connecticut, Delaware, Rhode Island, Vermont, and Hawaii. Another alternative that some jurisdictions are exploring is contracting out the operation of jails to private firms. In a few areas of the country, this recent for-profit approach is becoming increasingly popular. No longer is private contracting limited to a few functions that jails are not well equipped to handle, such as food or medical services. Throughout the country, private contracting historically has been found more often in juvenile and community-based facilities than in adult detention. But today there is a very significant movement in many states to contract the prison construction and operation to private companies. Some of these companies include Wackenhut Corrections, Corrections Corporation of America, and Esmor Correctional Services, to name a few. In all cases, as the available contracts increase, employment opportunities will continue to expand. Although technically the private corporation would be the employer, there would still be job requirements as established by that state. Thus applicants will still be screened and trained according to prevailing standards.

Pretrial release, home detention, electronic surveillance, and private contracting are among the options correctional administrators have explored to cope with a continually growing inmate population. But the most frequent response by far has been construction of new jails and prisons, which is occurring at a pace unprecedented in the history of corrections. The observation that there are fewer jails now than there were several years ago, possibly a loss of some eighty per year, does not impact negatively on job opportunities.

The larger regional jails, being built in such states as Virginia, West Virginia, and Kentucky, all will employ more officers and specialists than some of those smaller jails ever did. Many of these construction projects involve new-generation facilities. As described by the National Institute of Corrections,[1] new-generation facilities can be compared to the next generation of computers, whose capabilities improve with each new model. They are designed on the basis of state-of-the-art concepts developed by architects and psychologists about how institutions affect human behavior. New-generation structures are physically constructed to increase safety and security through architectural design, while at the same time, providing more humane living conditions. In con-

---

[1]This discussion of new-generation facilities has been summarized from the National Institute of Corrections' publication entitled *New Generation Jails: An Innovative Approach to an Age-Old Problem* by Stephen H. Gettinger (March 1984). It is available free of cost from the National Institute of Corrections, Longmont, Colorado 80501.

trast to older institutions, where cell bars separated officers from inmates, officers directly supervise inmates in new-generation facilities with no physical barriers between them. It is for this reason that the new-generation concept is also called "direct supervision."

Rather than patrolling corridors, direct supervision officers are stationed in a dormitory-style living area, where they directly control privileges, enforce rules and regulations, and closely supervise the inmate population. This is a dramatic change from traditional facility design, where an officer's ability to control inmates is more limited because there is less opportunity for contact and interaction. Largely because of the more pleasant atmosphere, these new-generation facilities have been found to reduce such traditional problems as tension, violence, noise, and idleness. Since inmates tend to take more pride in their living conditions, vandalism is rare, and peer pressure keeps the physical environment in good condition. There is also considerably more freedom of movement, as well as inmate access to telephones, recreation, and TV. Thus, there is a subtle pressure to conform to institutional rules and regulations to avoid losing these privileges.

Although officers are at first sometimes resistant to the direct inmate contact required in new-generation facilities, most overcome any initial reservations after working in such a setting. When they realize that they have more authority, fewer inmate disciplinary problems, less concern for personal safety, and greater opportunities to participate in management decisions, the officers themselves often become strong advocates for the direct supervision approach. Moreover, correctional systems that are building new-generation institutions tend to place a substantial emphasis on training officers in direct supervision techniques and interpersonal communication skills.

Although "new generation" represents the state-of-the-art in corrections, it is only in recent years that this trend has begun to influence the field. As new building projects are undertaken, there will undoubtedly be more direct supervision models. Although the vast majority of existing correctional systems reflect older designs, new-generation facilities can now be found in many major metropolitan areas—New York, Buffalo, Chicago, San Diego, San Jose, Tucson, Las Vegas, Portland, Miami, Tampa, Alexandria (Virginia), Contra Costa (California), and Prince Georges County (Maryland). As in most correctional institutions—whether new generation or not—tours are available upon request. Those seeking employment in correctional facilities are therefore encouraged to contact the nearest local, state, or federal facility and arrange a tour to get a firsthand view of working conditions and officer duties.

Of the approximately two hundred thousand local and four hundred thousand state correctional employees, the majority is in the classification of correctional officer. Salaries vary greatly for these sworn, uniformed officers, tending to increase with the size of the facility at the local level and to be standardized throughout the state for state employees (although cost-of-living differentials are sometimes provided in metropolitan areas). Starting levels tend to be around $28,000 for state officers. With overtime, night differential for evening shifts, and regular increases, an average correctional officer is probably earning in the $28,000 to $31,000 range. The current starting salary for state officers assigned to southeast Florida is $27,500. In some jurisdictions, collective bargaining units have successfully obtained pay parity with law enforcement officers, so salaries in heavily unionized sections of the country tend to be closer to that listed previously for police officers. In addition, large mega-jail systems generally compensate quite well. For example,

Miami-Dade County (Florida) maintains a sworn correctional officer staff of approximately sixteen hundred and offers a starting salary of about $29,000, depending on shift assignment, with the potential of advancing to $30,000 to $32,000 in this entry-level rank. Among other large county jail systems salaries are equally attractive: $32,000, Los Angeles; $30,500, Chicago; $30,000, San Francisco; $29,000, Seattle. Of course, jurisdictions with higher starting salaries are also likely to be more selective. In addition to traditional age, citizenship, and physical requirements, applicants should expect a polygraph examination, extensive background investigation, reading and writing tests, physical agility assessment, and/or psychological examination. A medical history, including a drug test, can be expected as well.

Probation and Parole

Career opportunities in corrections extend beyond secure institutions. Some offenders leave the courtroom and are placed on probation, which does not entail any form of confinement. Others, released after serving part of their sentence, are on parole or some other form of supervised release.

More than seventy-two thousand employees work in probation or parole, and they are about evenly divided between state and local jurisdictions. Salaries vary greatly for these correctional employees, nearly all of whom are college graduates. Compensation reflects the prevailing wages in the area where they are employed—which could be $26,000 for a juvenile court counselor, or as high as $40,000 for an experienced parole supervisor. Much depends upon the type of agency one is serving, and the types of client caseloads to be assigned.

Probation officers (sometimes called agents) have responsibility for compiling presentence investigations for the court. This officer may also be asked to make a formal court report and a recommendation to the judge for case disposition. In some locales there are investigators who conduct such investigations and compile information for the probation officer. Regardless of the size and volume of the jurisdiction, however, the probation officer is the professional responsible for advising and counseling the caseload of individuals placed on probation by the court. This counseling includes personal matters, social adjustment, work and economic circumstances, and all areas that would influence the required adjustment of the offender.

A recent survey of probation and parole agency directors cited increasing caseloads and workload management as by far the most critical concern. These same directors were especially concerned about the adequacy of substance abuse programs and the heavier caseloads that are due to increases in substance abuse without accompanying resources. Other special concerns expressed by these probation and parole directors were the need for more intensive monitoring of clients with mental illness, more treatment capacities for sex offenders, and the importance of expanding electronic monitoring in all jurisdictions.

In addition to counseling, job placement, and traditional social work–oriented functions, probation officers must enforce the rules imposed on the client by the court. Conditions of probation could include regular school attendance, abstinence from alcohol and/or drugs, participation in treatment programs, adherence to curfew hours, refraining from criminal associations, and the like. Thus, many probation officers find their role requires a delicate balance of social worker and rule enforcer. Some jurisdictions use teams of specialized officers, with one employee responsible for counseling, another for developing community contacts, and another for violation enforcement. But this approach is relatively unique, and it is far more common to find all of these tasks included in the combined function of one single probation officer.

Probation work exists with both juveniles and adults, and in all cases a plan must be formulated for directing and enforcing an effective rehabilitation arrangement. Much of the work of a probation officer involves contact with family, employers, and others whose lives affect the person on probation. Anyone interested in probation as a career would usually possess a bachelor's degree in the social sciences, human behavior, or criminal justice. At the graduate level, a master's degree is often required for supervisory duties and promotion. That degree might be in social work or in a field that relates closely to understanding and influencing human behavior.

Parole officers do much the same type of work and have many of the same kinds of responsibilities. However, their clientele have already served time in institutions and have been released conditionally on parole. Hence, the parolee may require more intensive supervision, and, in some cases, group therapy and other behavior adjustment techniques. The parole officer may have to arrange for the client to find either a place to live or a job and will also have to enforce the specific conditions of release.

There are various opportunities for advancement and career development in both probation and parole, including intensive caseloads for therapy and counseling purposes, field supervisors, office managers, and district or regional administrators. These positions function at federal and state levels, as well as local and county levels. They also service juveniles, young adults, and adult offenders. There are institutional parole officers, whose tasks involve assisting the inmate prior to early release or supervising the adjustment process for those about to be released. Although caseloads tend to be high, the work is challenging and rewarding. An excellent way to learn more about this field is to ask to perform an internship as part of the college educational experience. Many probation and parole offices welcome college students who can assist in investigations and participate in basic offender supervision work.

Additional Correctional Opportunities

Within this extensive field ranging from pretrial services to probation, custody, treatment, rehabilitation, and parole, there are many additional jobs that have not been discussed. For example, in correctional facilities numerous employment possibilities exist beyond the correctional officer. These include the living unit supervisor (cottage parent), the various industry shop supervisors, those involved in inmate reception and classification, and a variety of special assignments related to counseling, treatment, record keeping, and maintenance of the institution. In the latter case, the facility may be a farm, a lumber camp, or a unit assigned to road construction and repair. In such types of correctional units, the officer often doubles as job supervisor and personal counselor.

The list of the correctional personnel categories in Appendix B demonstrates the variety of job opportunities within the field. This list is an excellent indication of the number of trained staff required to effectively administer programs in criminal justice. Some serve at the beginning of the process, as in the case of gang workers in social agencies; some are employed in the pretrial phase; and others are utilized to administer the correctional system either in institutions or through such community-based processes as probation and parole. But, as we have repeatedly stressed, everyone in corrections is looking for talented and energetic, young, career-minded men and women.

Criminalistics and the Crime Lab

The career field that is perhaps most directly related to enforcement but that occurs in the laboratory and not on the street, is called criminalistics, or forensic science. There are several paths into this scientific area, depending on the specialty. Most frequently the criminalist is someone who majored in chemistry or physics and who has experience in applying this scientific competence to physical evidence and the questions of the criminal investigator. Here is where the crime scene puzzles of how, what, when, and where can be answered.

The criminalist obtains experience through an internship while in college, and later, while employed in a crime laboratory. Because of the shortage of qualified persons in criminalistics, particularly those with graduate degrees, there are also opportunities to become a director of such a lab. Some criminalists prefer not to become involved in the administrative duties of a lab director, however, and therefore are employed as scientists engaged in the critical task of analyzing physical evidence and determining facts through their highly technical knowledge.

The forensic scientist is a more highly skilled and specialized scientific investigator in a single area of physical evidence analysis. As such, the forensic scientist generally is not as concerned with all physical/legal aspects of evidence as is the criminalist. The services of both are crucial to the enforcement agencies, as well as to the defense. Opportunities are always available for those who prepare for such careers through a background in the natural and physical sciences.

As with general enforcement work, there are laboratories at all jurisdictional levels. Some federal agencies have extensive facilities. Most notable are those of the FBI, Drug Enforcement Administration, and Post Office departments. Most states have labs serving the headquarters of their state enforcement unit in addition to other state labs that provide testing services primarily for the regulatory units in state government. Most major cities also have crime labs. Others, frequently known as regional forensic labs, assist local departments in their entire region, so there are a number of locations for such employment.

In addition to the work of the chemist and physicist, there are lab staffing needs in such fields as the polygraph (lie detector), the examination of questioned documents, fingerprint identification, and ballistics (firearms and tool identification), all of which require personal experience following considerable on-the-job training. Once the examiner qualifies as an expert, much of his or her time is spent testifying in court. If one has a scientific and inquisitive mind, the work of the criminalist or laboratory-forensic examiner beckons.

The criminalist or forensic scientist, whether a biologist, chemist, or physicist, conducts tests related to a specialized area of science. The chemist may make determinations as to whether a stain is truly blood, whether a pill contains a narcotic drug, or whether a paint chip came from a particular automobile fender. The work of the forensic chemist has expanded greatly with the utilization of DNA testing for matching of fluids. The physicist may make analyses of metals, glass, or other suspect materials. Their primary concern in testing is to establish positive identifications and relationships to crimes, and their findings may determine a suspect's innocence or guilt. The work of the forensic scientist has become more recognized and more demanded, due to the requirements of the courts for tangible and factual evidence and on the part of the public, which has grown up on television shows depicting the scientific investigation of crime.

There is optimism about the job market for the forensic science specialist because surveys indicate that more than five hundred new people are needed each year. Since nationwide there are only some twenty graduate programs in the forensic sciences, there continue to be vacancies for qualified individuals. Salaries range from $45,000 to $55,000 for those with scientific educational preparation and will be greater with experience and in the largest laboratories, such as the federal agency labs. A major crime lab director can readily reach $100,000 in salary with teaching and expert witness consulting as extra.

Forensic science, therefore, is a broad field in which physical and biological sciences are used to analyze and evaluate physical evidence related to law. Physical evidence is any physical item with potential for providing information to the criminal justice system, civil litigation, or other matters of public safety interest and concern. In addition to criminalists, forensic pathologists, and forensic toxicologists, these sciences include document examiners, anthropologists, psychiatrists, and a variety of chemists and physicists. Some departments and laboratories employ technicians who are skilled in certain instrumentation, but not necessarily in all aspects of the scientific profession. In preparation, one would normally follow a course of study through chemistry, instrumental analysis and microscopy, other sciences such as biology and physics as they relate to physical evidence, and selected legal courses. There are even forensic entomologists who determine periods of time through the decaying process and insect infestation.

For technician positions, one should complete as much high school math and science as possible and then look to more basic sciences in the community college. More and more departments now employ personnel under the titles of "crime scene technician," "lab technician," or "crime analyst." These jobs may require high school graduation, and further academic study is encouraged after employment. Positions such as identification technician provide excellent experience and training on-the-job in photography, evidence collection, preparing reports, and classifying fingerprints while permitting access to higher education as well.

Let us review some of the specialized examiners and scientists who are found within the forensic laboratory.

The Polygraph Operator and the Document Examiner

The polygraph operator, or lie detector examiner, should have a working knowledge of human behavior and of physiological and psychological responses in humans. Through skillful testing of victims, suspects, witnesses, and others, this person is often able to determine whether an individual's verbal responses are truthful. The process of getting truthful responses is a delicate one, and the examiner must have a sound knowledge of both personality differences and interviewing techniques. Again, and most importantly, the polygraph operator may determine one's lack of involvement in a particular criminal situation.

The document examiner has a variety of skills and tools with which to work. This specialist may be called on to analyze the signature on a check or compare known samples of a suspect's handwriting with a ransom note or other suspicious document. In a more mechanical way, the document examiner may be asked to find out if a particular typewriter was used in the preparation of a deceased person's final will or whether the age of the ink and the age of the paper correspond on an alleged valuable document.

Document examiners deal with questions that need not always be criminal matters. One might be asked to help resolve cases involving the ages of conflicting or contested wills. Or one might be asked to resolve questions of signature authenticity in autographs, property deeds, and ownership titles.

Fingerprint and Firearms Expert

The expert in fingerprint identification begins to obtain experience by classifying and comparing the many fingerprints on file in both criminal and noncriminal record systems. After considerable experience in making positive identifications and testifying to these in court, an examiner may become regarded as an expert. The importance of this means of identification cannot be overstressed, since it continues to be our most positive single means of providing proof of individual identity. (DNA may someday replace fingerprints when sufficient numbers of the population are in a data bank.) The expert in this field also will be called upon to make determinations in the case of footprints, palm prints, and other less common but equally positive sources.

The firearms identification expert is most frequently portrayed firing a revolver into a container and then making microscopic comparisons of the bullet in order to discover whether that particular weapon fired the suspect bullet. Although such activities occupy some time, this specialist also is asked questions about whether a certain piece of metal came in contact with a specific door of a safe, or if a suspected burglary tool can positively be placed at the scene of a known break-in. The expert may also determine the distance of a shot that was fired, the direction from which a bullet came, and what type of weapon was presumably used in a crime. The firearms expert deals with more than guns; all types of weapons and metal instruments are tested and compared.

The Lab Technician

The increased demand in recent years for analysis of blood, drugs, and alcohol has highlighted the importance of a well-staffed laboratory. As has been pointed out by the Supreme Court, the police must rely more on scientifically determined physical evidence than on suspects' confessions.

In the crime laboratory, there are employment possibilities as a laboratory technician. Technicians' specific duties depend on the area of the lab in which they function, and it is possible, through continuing formal education and on-the-job experience, to become an examiner and, ultimately, an expert in the field. Otherwise there would be little potential for advancement in this highly specialized setting.

Outside of the laboratory, careers exist in the field of identifying physical evidence. Evidence technicians are primarily responsible for the collection and packaging of all physical evidence at the crime scene and are expected to be proficient in the use of photographic equipment and in making sketches and plaster casts. The evidence technician, then, is responsible for the proper identification of suspicious items at the crime scene and for their safe delivery to the laboratory examiner.

More and more, lab work is being done in mobile crime laboratories, and this will demand more field personnel to inspect crime scenes, collect items for analysis, and perform necessary tests for later court presentation.

Some evidence technicians are police officers; some are civilians. The vehicles they use are equipped with everything from illumination devices to facilities for field analyses of various kinds. They take photographs, make plaster and plastic casts, search out fingerprints and other forms of offender traces, and operate a vacuum to collect hairs and fibers. They must be able to collect and preserve properly any significant finding.

Forensic chemists, the most common laboratory professionals, are responsible for determining any connections that exist between case evidence and suspects. They conduct microscopic examinations and chemical tests on materials such as hair, fibers, skin, paint, glass, dirt, poisons, drugs, fabrics, gases, and substances of all types. Most of these tests, known as X-ray spectrometers, chromatography, ultraviolet and infrared spectrometers, and microphotography, analyze unknown substances to determine and identify any significance to a crime. These chemists will be called upon to ascertain if a located sample is blood and if so, what type, and any other factors that can be indicated from that sample. Other body fluids (DNA) can also be evaluated for positive links to offenders, victims, and suspects. Many new techniques have been introduced into the modern crime lab, and precision instruments such as electronic cell counters and electronic microscopes demand both formal training and experience on the job. For one who has persistence and not just patience, a talent for scientific inquiry, and a determination that can overcome the unpleasant odors, sights, and other frustrations, the employment outlook is quite favorable in the forensic lab, and it is projected to continue to be so for the foreseeable future. The programs in universities are limited in number, and they can be lengthy when one combines legal knowledge, scientific studies, and investigative skills with the required internship in a lab.

A specialist position not affiliated with the crime laboratory, but one with technical expertise in receiving, analyzing, and assessing criminal information, is the crime analyst. These personnel receive confidential information and analyze data, prepare reports, and disseminate information to assist in criminal investigations or intelligence assessments. Their unique type of work involves studying criminal groups, methods of operations, and extent of criminal influences, and making recommendations for investigative strategies and long-range planning.

All of the personnel in this section—as is the case with detectives and investigators—must have an ability to evaluate, analyze, and present information accurately. They must communicate clearly and have the capacity to apply logic and sound judgment to criminal operations. The ability to prepare reports and illustrative devices and to use data to one's advantage is paramount. Computer skills, too, are essential, as analysts monitor a variety of sources of data and statistics. They are particularly vital when reviewing computer crimes, fraudulent schemes, organized crime, and business-related criminal enterprises.

Private Security, Loss Prevention, and Risk Management

Yearly crime-related losses to the business, retail, and industrial community total more than an estimated one hundred billion dollars a year. This figure includes employee theft and embezzlement and customer shoplifting. The market for an alternative to public policing has been growing rapidly. Over twelve million businesses and commercial establishments, from Fortune 500 companies to neighborhood markets, recognize that the half-million-plus public police personnel are not sufficient to provide the necessary protection. This flourishing industry has grown at a 10 to 12 percent rate since the 1970s, and it is now a $60 billion dollar industry.

Estimates currently place the number of private security employees at 1.6 million, making them far larger than the public sector. In terms of employment, and in terms of dollar amounts actually expended on protection, the private sector is ahead. This would include contracted closed-circuit and alarm monitoring services as well as more traditional armored cars and uniformed officers.

Estimates as to the number of firms and companies that provide various forms of security and protection are approximately twelve thousand. Many of these companies are one-person firms owned by a former police or military officer. Since corporate America is so much more security-conscious today, there will continue to be as much as a 20 percent growth in demand annually for employment within this marketplace.

Locations to be serviced range from colleges to hotels, from airports to museums, from subway systems to financial institutions; and the requirements and rewards are just as varied. Twenty-three states have now enacted standards and training legislation, and as these training requirements increase, so will the salaries. Presently an armed and trained private security officer can expect to earn between $1,500 and $2,000 per month. A medium-sized organization will pay $45,000 to $50,000 per year for its director of security. The national average for all private security directors today is $55,000. The highest director salaries are in utilities and manufacturing companies.

Recent studies indicate that well over 1.6 million persons are employed within the framework of private industrial and retail security work. This can range from traditional guards, who are responsible for security in buildings and grounds, to bank guards and railroad police and can extend into sophisticated assignments, such as insurance investigation and loss prevention specialists. Private security expenditures emphasize crime prevention through locks, alarms, patrol, TV surveillance, and other means of protecting persons and property.

The 1977 *National Task Force Report on Private Security* stated that the private security system, with more than one million workers at the time, sophisticated alarm systems and perimeter safeguards, armored trucks, advanced minicomputers, and thousands of highly skilled crime prevention experts, offers a potential for coping with crime that cannot be equaled by any other remedy or approach. Companies with the largest shares of the market and a history of solid performance include CPP/Pinkerton, Burns International Security Services, Wackenhut, Wells Fargo, Guardsmark, and American and Protective Services. Pinkerton and American are both based in California, and Wackenhut is in Florida. Brinks Incorporated, best known for its armored car service, also has home security services and twenty-four-hour alarm monitoring.

Pinkerton, originally founded by Allan Pinkerton, earned its reputation in the Old West. It is now a major firm with a workforce of fifty thousand and revenues of $800 million. This firm is well known to nearly everyone because of its uniformed guards and notices on display in stores and on doors and windows. It is also known through its company protection signs, armored trucks, residential security, and private contract investigations. Salaries and advancement potential vary greatly in such work, and an applicant would be well advised to first inquire about a firm's reputation, since most states do have requirements set for obtaining private licenses.

Some major corporations and businesses employ their own security forces. Employment therein usually is attractive and stable since such persons enjoy the benefits that accompany work in private industry. As concern over internal security, employee thefts, and inventory controls becomes more widespread, many companies are developing high-level, sophisticated security units to provide safety and security within their own facilities. These highly sophisticated security systems have to be monitored, and some industries have found it more efficient to outsource this work instead of employing their own staffs.

Like public peace officers, these employees may be provided with some enforcement powers and will possess communication equipment and weapons. Standards for such jobs are being raised, and the federal government has been encouraging states to initiate minimum standards for entrance into retail and industrial security work. (Persons interested should locate and review the Private Security Officers Quality Assurance Act of 1995.) Guardsmark, based in Tennessee and one of the largest security firms, enjoys a reputation for high-quality personnel and stringent requirements for employment.

As one might expect in the private sector, jobs at the top are competitive and well compensated. The proper combination of enforcement and investigative experience, coupled with higher education and some amount of management drive and skill, can lead to a high-salary position. Numerous former police chiefs from major cities serve as vice presidents for security and loss prevention with large corporations in the United States, and their salaries exceed those earned while they were municipal police chiefs.

Private sector security firms, such as Wackenhut, are moving into the prison business, too. A potential growth area will be the operating of detention and short-term lock-up facilities. Thus, along with protecting nuclear sites, power plants, embassies in foreign lands, and many global airports, there now is the business of constructing and operating jail and detention centers. A firm such as Wackenhut provides a most modern career opportunity by combining sophisticated training and protection duties at a nuclear reactor site or at utility-owned nuclear power plants. Such work goes a long way to dispel the image of private security employment as mere guard duty at minimum wage!

Department of Labor statistics for 1990 show that over 30 percent of new employees in security-related fields are females. That trend appears to be continuing and may even have been increased lately. The private sector has a history of employing women in security work that predates by half a century that of the public police, since it was Allan Pinkerton who hired women as early as the 1850s.

It can be expected that private sector security will continue to increase and expand, to strengthen its standards, and to increase its educational requirements. As computer theft becomes more common, there will be even greater efforts to counter such crime and to employ persons with unique sets of skills. "Cybercrime," as it has been labeled, has already expanded the need for specialists to track hackers and violators of Web integrity, investigate computer attacks and the illegal uses of systems and networks, and secure these systems from intentional damage or viruses. The future in this area is excellent, and one way to start is to obtain a uniformed officer security job during college. Working part-time, on varied shifts, even for modest wages, is a way to obtain the necessary experience and reputation for dependability and resourcefulness. Some colleges even have such employment available to students studying criminal justice. And at the same time, you can be studying computer sciences and information technology.

The stigma that has long plagued this industry is that security personnel were ill trained and received low wages. As the states enact selection and training requirements, the standards are rising, and background reviews, similar to those for public police, have become the law. Florida has passed a law requiring applicants for security licenses to complete twenty-four hours of training, plus twenty-eight hours for those seeking jobs that require carrying weapons.

The major firms can expect to employ personnel with police or military backgrounds, and the pay is likewise higher. These firms will provide more training than the law may require. The large firms also utilize a selective screening process that can include psychological, polygraph, and drug examinations. A wise decision in seeking such job employment or career opportunities will rest on the inquiries one makes. Thus, the state agency that licenses or regulates private security firms may be the place to start. College programs with security courses and police training centers are also sources of reliable information.

Supportive Jobs

In addition to the aforementioned related careers, there are numerous other opportunities for employment within enforcement agencies that can be referred to as supportive. In many departments, particularly the smaller ones, sworn personnel may perform some of these supportive jobs, but more and more, especially in large cities, they have become the responsibility of civilian personnel. Some of these services are related to communications, such as receiving incoming telephone calls, dispatching officers upon request, and obtaining complaints directly from citizens. Everyone is familiar with the critical role played by the 911 operator. Others relate to the immense record-keeping task, and included here are services related to accident reports, fingerprint classifications, criminal history files, and routine processing of reports and case files.

Another major responsibility of any police agency is the maintenance of all recovered property, and many hours are devoted to identifying such items as physical evidence, lost and found items, property owned by prisoners, seized assets, and impounded automobiles. Many departments employ data analysts who follow up on all reports submitted by officers and ensure their accuracy and proper completion. More recently this function has involved dealing with computers and providing statistical data. Such persons may also be termed "incident analysts" or "crime analysts."

Civilians also may be involved in public information, equipment maintenance, staff training, community relations, photography, classification and counseling in detention facilities, and such highly responsible duties as comprehensive planning and computer analysis of crime data. These jobs have been the result of federal government financial initiatives of the 1970s and 1980s that assisted local agencies by providing support for innovative and successful projects. A newly established career field, for example, is that of the planner in many agencies. Likewise, researchers and crime/incident analysts will continue to be needed to assist with long-range forecasting of needs and directions and to assist decision makers through evaluation. It was mentioned earlier, but the new career of victim's advocate has become a more frequently seen position in the justice system. Court administrators, legal advisors, crime mapping specialists, and the planner/analysts cited above were all the direct result of prior commission recommendations and federal funding.

In addition, there are the previously mentioned relatively new roles of community service officers, public service aides, and other nonsworn personnel. These positions, which often involve taking complaints and reporting traffic problems and accidents, appeal to persons who aspire to work in police departments but not as sworn officers. Of course, it is not uncommon for some public service officers to choose law enforcement as a career, particularly after they have pursued part or all of a college education.

Civilian positions may appeal to the young person who is interested in employment within the criminal justice system but who is unable to meet stringent physical or other qualifications for patrol duty. Or they may appeal to students who majored in business, economics, planning, computer science, physical sciences, information systems, or other disciplines that relate to the justice and safety systems. Civilian assignments also may be provided to former officers who are injured or disabled.

Summary

A career in law enforcement/public safety is one of the most challenging in our complex society, and the demands made upon the law enforcement officer are so great that only those with excellent qualifications—physical, mental, and emotional—are selected.

As the President's Crime Commission stated in the *Task Force Report [on the] Police* in 1967:

> The demands upon police are likely to increase in number and complexity in the years ahead, and dealing adequately with current law enforcement needs requires a clear acknowledgment that police are one of the most important governmental administrative agencies in evidence today.

Not only are the police an essential governmental agency, the makeup of enforcement personnel is even more important. As the National Advisory Commission on Criminal Justice Standards and Goals noted in 1973 regarding the needs of police personnel:

> The police service must recruit and employ the caliber of personnel that are now found within our colleges and universities, those possessing intellectual curiosity, analytical ability, articulateness, and a capacity to relate the events of the day to the social, political, and historical context in which they occur.

In conclusion, a career in law enforcement can provide a rewarding opportunity for young men and women who believe that they would like to be in the most stimulating and unpredictable of the human service occupations. As in all other human services, the greatest rewards come in the form of personal satisfaction. No career can be more important to a democracy than one that protects all citizens and is the recognized symbol of justice under our laws.

8

NATIONAL ASSOCIATIONS

THERE ARE A number of national organizations that provide information and materials to persons interested in justice related careers. There are also a number of federal agencies that provide career information directly and whose service also includes publications and informational handouts. All will likely have websites that you should look to for more information.

Some of the national associations and organizations are listed below:

International Association of Chiefs of Police
515 N. Washington St.
Alexandria, VA 22314-2357

This large membership organization provides training courses, written materials, and a variety of other services to its members and others. The Education and Training Committee links the IACP with colleges, training academies, and the resources being produced by commercial firms.

Academy of Criminal Justice Sciences
7319 Hanover Pkwy.
Greenbelt, MD 20770

Established in 1963 as the International Association of Police Professors, the Academy has broadened its base and changed its name. It is designed to further communication and research among academic personnel concerned with the many issues involved in the criminal justice professions and their relationship with higher education. Student memberships are encouraged.

National Council on Crime & Delinquency
1970 Broadway, Ste. 500
Oakland, CA 94612

NCCD is a nonprofit citizen organization supported by contributions and foundations. It works to improve the criminal justice system and to maximize the effectiveness of all agencies within that system. It is especially concerned with stimulating community programs for the prevention, treatment, and control of delinquency and crime.

National Sheriffs' Association
1450 Duke St.
Alexandria, VA 22314-3490

NSA is a membership organization dedicated to furthering the goals of the Office of the Sheriff and the professional services that it represents. Career information may be available, as well as historical insights and current descriptive articles.

Lambda Alpha Epsilon
American Criminal Justice Association
P.O. Box 61047
Sacramento, CA 95860

This student/alumni organization offers a timely and informative journal. Write for information about the organization and its purpose. The membership fraternity, formed in San Jose, California, in 1937, welcomes pre-service students as well as those already employed in the justice field. Chapters are located across the country in colleges with active criminal justice education programs. Regional chapters hold regular meetings and provide newsletters.

American Jail Association
2053 Day Rd., Ste. 100
Hagerstown, MD 27140-9795

National Institute of Justice
National Criminal Justice Reference Service
U.S. Department of Justice
Washington, DC 20531

Write for reference material and resources. This office will respond to specific inquiries at (800) 851-3420.

Other helpful associations include:

International Association of Women Police
R.R.#1, Box #149
Deer Isle, ME 04627

American Correctional Association
4380 Forbes Blvd.
Lanham, MD 20706-4322

American Society of Criminology
Ohio State University Research
1314 Kinnear Rd., Ste. 212
Columbus, OH 43212

American Society for Industrial Security
1625 Prince St.
Alexandria, VA 22314-2818

Fraternal Order of Police
1410 Donelson Pike, #A17
Nashville, TN 37217

Police Executive Research Forum
1120 Connecticut Ave. NW, Ste. 930
Washington, DC 20036

Office of Fire Prevention & Arson Control
National Emergency Training Center
16825 S. Seton Ave.
Emmitsburg, MD 21727

National League of Cities
1301 Pennsylvania Ave. NW
Washington, DC 20004

Office of International Criminal Justice
University of Illinois
1333 S. Wabash Ave.
Chicago, IL 60605

National Association of Counties
440 First St. NW
Washington, DC 20001

American Probation & Parole Association
P.O. Box 11910
Lexington, KY 40578-1910

National Organization for Victim Assistance
1730 Park Rd. NW
Washington, DC 20010

Additionally, each state has its own chiefs of police association, sheriff's association, and local chapters of the American Society for Industrial Security. There are also state chapters that are affiliates of the American Correctional Association, and others on the list, in many states. Many such organizations provide employment information or career guidance if at all possible; some maintain a permanent staff for such services.

In addition to the Federal Office of Personnel Management, there are regional federal job information/testing offices in most states and in most major cities. Some states such as California, New York, Pennsylvania, and Texas have several locations. Contact these regional offices for job specific information, forms, and testing requirements on federal positions.

The following are job posting websites that one should know about and use as appropriate:

National Criminal Justice Reference Service: ncjrs.org/index.html
University of North Texas: unt.edu.cjus/employ/htm
Job Hotlines USA: careers.org/topic/01-002.html
Michigan State University: lib.msu.edu/harris23/ crimjust/jobs.htm
Frank Schmalleger: talkjustice.com
North Carolina Wesleyan College: http://faculty.ncwc. edu/toconnor/employ.htm
The Corrections Connection: corrections.com
Law Enforcement Jobs Employment Portal: lawenforcementjob.com
The Blue Line Jobs Page: theblueline.com
policeemployment.com
prisonguard.com

Federal Bureau of Prisons: Regional Locations

Mid-Atlantic Region

Regional Office
Junction Business Park
10010 Junction Dr., Ste. 100 N
Annapolis Junction, MD 20701

North Central Region

Regional Office
Gateway Complex Tower II, 8th Fl.
Fourth and State Ave.
Kansas City, KS 66101

Northeast Region

Regional Office
U.S. Customs House, 7th Fl.
Second and Chestnut Sts.
Philadelphia, PA 19106

South Central Region

Regional Office
4211 Cedar Springs Rd., Ste. 300
Dallas TX 75129

Southeast Region

Regional Office
3800 North Camp Creek Pkwy. SW, Bldg. 2000
Atlanta, GA 30331

Western Region

Regional Office
7950 Dublin Blvd., 3rd Fl.
Dublin, CA 94002

Central Offices

National Recruitment Office
320 First St. NW, Rm. 460
Washington, DC 20534

Medical Recruitment
320 First St. NW, Rm. 1034
Washington, DC 20534

Staffing Office
320 First St. NW, Rm. 400
Washington, DC 20534

Federal Bureau of Prisons
Examining Section (for Correctional Officers only)
10010 Junction Dr., Ste. 217 S
Annapolis Junction, MD 20701

Federal Bureau of Prisons
Examining Section (for Psychologists, Medical Officers, Physician
    Assistants, Correctional Treatment and Drug Treatment
    Specialists only)
320 First St. NW, Rm. 460
Washington, DC 20534

APPENDIX B

State Adult Departments of Corrections

INDIVIDUAL STATE ADULT departments of corrections can be found at the following addresses:

Alabama
101 S. Union St.
P.O. Box 301501
Montgomery, AL 36130
(334) 353-3870
agencies.state.al.us/doc

Alaska
240 Main St., Ste. 700
Juneau, AK 99801
(907) 465-4652
correct.state.ak.us

Arizona
1601 W. Jefferson
Phoenix, AZ 85007
(602) 542-5497
http://adcprisoninfo.az.gov

Arkansas
6814 Princeton Pike
P.O. Box 8707
Pine Bluff, AR 71602
(870) 267-6200
state.ar.us/doc

California
1515 S St.
P.O. Box 942883
Sacramento, CA 94283
(916) 445-7688
cdc.state.ca.us

Colorado
2862 S Circle Dr., Ste. 400
Colorado Spring, CO 80906
(719) 579-9580
doc.state.co.us

Connecticut
24 Walcott Hill Rd.
Wethersfield, CT 06109
(860) 692-7492
state.ct.us/doc

Delaware
245 McKee Rd.
Dover, DE 19904
(302) 739-5601
state.de.us/correct

District of Columbia
1923 Vermont Ave. NW
Washington, DC 20001
(202) 673-7316
http://doc.dc.gov

Florida
2601 Blair Stone Rd.
Tallahassee, FL 32399
(850) 488-7480
dc.state.fl.us

Georgia
2 Martin Luther King Jr. Dr. SE
Twin Towers E, Ste. 866
Atlanta, GA 30334
(404) 656-6002
dcor.state.ga.us

Hawaii
919 Ala Moana Blvd.
Honolulu, HI 96814
(808) 587-1350
state.hi.us/icsd/psd/psd.html

Idaho
1299 N. Orchard St., Ste. 110
Boise, ID 83706
(208) 658-2000
corr.state.id.us

Illinois
1301 Concordia Ct.
P.O. Box 19277
Springfield, IL 62794
(217) 522-2666
idoc.state.il.us

Indiana
Government Center South
302 W. Washington St., Rm. E334
Indianapolis, IN 46204
(317) 232-5715
state.in.us/indcorrection

Iowa
420 Watson Powell Jr. Way
Des Moines, IA 50309
(515) 242-5703
doc.state.ia.us

Kansas
Landon State Office Bldg.
900 SW Jackson, 4th Fl.
Topeka, KS 66612
(785) 296-3317
http://docnet.dc.state.ks.us

Kentucky
P.O. Box 2400
Frankfort, KY 40602
(502) 564-4726
cor.state.ky.us

Louisiana
504 Mayflower St.
P.O. Box 94304
Baton Rouge, LA 70802
(225) 342-6741
corrections.state.la.us

Maine
State House Station 111
Augusta, ME 04333
(207) 287-4360
http://janus.state.me.us/corrections

Maryland
6776 Reistertown Rd., Ste. 310
Baltimore, MD 21215
(410) 585-3300
dpscs.state.md.us/doc

Massachusetts
50 Maple St., Ste. 3
Milford, MA 01757
(508) 422-3339
state.ma.us/doc

Michigan
Grandview Plaza Bldg.
P.O. Box 30003
Lansing, MI 48909
(517) 373-0720
state.mi.us/mdoc

Minnesota
1450 Energy Park Dr., Ste. 200
St. Paul, MN 55108
(651) 642-0282
doc.state.mn.us

Mississippi
723 N. President St.
Jackson, MS 39202
(601) 359-5600
mdoc.state.ms.us

Missouri
2729 Plaza Dr.
P.O. Box 236
Jefferson City, MO 65102
(573) 751-2389
corrections.state.mo.us

Montana
1539 11th Ave.
P.O. Box 201301
Helena, MT 59620
(406) 444-3930
cor.state.mt.us

Nebraska
Folsom and W Prospector Pl., Bldg. 1
P.O. Box 94661
Lincoln, NE 68522
(402) 471-2654
corrections.state.ne.us

Nevada
5500 Snyder Ave., Bldg. 89
P.O. Box 7011
Carson City, NV 89701
(775) 887-3216
prisons.state.nv.us

New Hampshire
105 Pleasant St.
P.O. Box 1806
Concord, NH 03302
(603) 271-5600
state.nh.us/doc

New Jersey
Whittlesey Rd.
P.O. Box 863
Trenton, NJ 08625
(609) 292-4036
state.nj.us/corrections

New Mexico
4337 New Mexico 14
P.O. Box 27116
Santa Fe, NM 87505
(505) 827-8709
state.nm.us/corrections

New York
1220 Washington Ave., Bldg. 2
Albany, NY 12226
(518) 457-8126
docs.state.ny.us

North Carolina
214 W. Jones St., MSC 4201
Raleigh, NC 27699
(919) 716-3700
doc.state.nc.us

North Dakota
3303 E. Main
P.O. Box 1898
Bismarck, ND 58502
(701) 328-6390
state.nd.us/docr

Ohio
1050 Freeway Dr. N
Columbus, OH 43229
(614) 752-1164
drc.state.oh.us

Oklahoma
3400 Martin Luther King Ave.
P.O. Box 11400
Oklahoma City, OK 73136
(405) 425-2505
doc.state.ok.us

Oregon
2575 Center St. NE
Salem, OR 97301
(503) 945-0920
doc.state.or.us

Pennsylvania
2520 Lisburn Rd.
P.O. Box 598
Camp Hill, PA 17001
(717) 975-4918
cor.state.pa.us

Rhode Island
40 Howard Ave.
Cranston, RI 02920
(401) 462-2611
doc.state.ri.us

South Carolina
4444 Broad River Rd.
P.O. Box 21787
Columbia, SC 29221
(803) 896-8555
state.sc.us/scdc

South Dakota
3200 E. Hwy. 34
c/o 500 E. Capitol Ave.
Pierre, SD 57501
(605) 773-3478
state.sd.us/corrections/corrections

Tennessee
320 6th Ave. N, 4th Fl.
Nashville, TN 37243
(615) 741-1000
state.tn.us/correction

Texas
Spur 59 off Hwy. 75 N
P.O. Box 99
Huntsville, TX 77342
(936) 437-2101
tdcj.state.tx.us

Utah
14717 S. Minuteman Dr.
Draper, UT 84020
(801) 545-5500
udc.state.ut.us

Vermont
103 S. Main St.
Waterbury, VT 05671
(802) 241-2442
doc.state.vt.us

Virginia
6900 Atmore Dr.
P.O. Box 26963
Richmond, VA 23261
(804) 674-3119
vadoc.state.va.us

Washington
410 W. 5th Ave.
P.O. Box 41100
Olympia, WA 98504
(360) 753-1573
wa.gov/doc

West Virginia
112 California Ave.
Bldg. 4, Rm. 300
Charleston, WV 25305
(304) 558-2036
state.wv.us/wvdoc

Wisconsin
3099 E. Washington Ave.
P.O. Box 7925
Madison, WI 53707
(608) 240-5055
wi-doc.com

Wyoming
700 W. 21st St.
Cheyenne, WY 82002
(307) 777-7208
http://doc.state.wy.us

Recommended Reading

THE JOURNALS AND textbooks listed here are good sources of information for those interested in reading about law enforcement issues.

Journals and Other Sources

American Jails
2053 Day Rd., Ste. 100
Hagerstown, MD 21740-9795

Corrections Today
American Correctional Association
4380 Forbes Blvd.
Lanham, MD 20706-4322

Crime & Delinquency
National Council on Crime & Delinquency
Sage Publications, Inc.
2111 W. Hillcrest Dr.
Newbury Park, CA 91320

Criminal Justice International
Office of International Criminal Justice
University of Illinois at Chicago
715 S. Wood
Chicago, IL 60612

Criminology
American Society of Criminology
1314 Kinnear Rd., Ste. 212
Columbus, OH 43212

FBI Law Enforcement Bulletin
Federal Bureau of Investgation
U.S. Department of Justice
Washington, DC 20535

Federal Employees Almanac
Federal Employees News Digest, Inc.
1850 Centennial Park Dr., Ste. 520
Reston, VA 20191
(publishes books, newsletters, and information on federal
   government employment)

Journal of Criminal Justice
Pergamon Press
P.O. Box 945
New York, NY 10010

Journal of Forensic Sciences
American Academy of Forensic Sciences
225 S. Academy Blvd.
Colorado Springs, CO 80910

Journal of Police Science & Administration
International Association of Chiefs of Police
515 N. Washington St.
Alexandria, VA 22314-2357

Journal of Security Administration
Academy of Security Educators & Trainers
30 Falcon Dr.
Hauppauge, NY 11788

Law and Order Magazine
(product and news publication for the police market)
lawandordermag.com

National Sheriff
1400 Duke St.
Alexandria, VA 22314

Police Chief
International Association of Chiefs of Police
515 N. Washington St.
Alexandria, VA 22314-2357

Security Management
American Society for Industrial Security
1625 Prince St.
Alexandria, VA 22314

Security World (newsletter)
securityworld.com

Criminal Justice Textbooks

Abadinsky, H. *Probation & Parole*. Upper Saddle River, NJ: Prentice Hall, 1999.

Abadinsky, H., and L. T. Winfree. *Criminal Justice, An Introduction*. Chicago: Nelson Hall Publishers, 1992.

Adams, Thomas F. *Police Field Operations*, 5th ed. Upper Saddle River, NJ: Prentice Hall, 2000.

Albanese, Jay, and Robert Pursley. *Crime in America*. Upper Saddle River, NJ: Prentice Hall, 1998.

Barker, T., R. Hunter, and J. Rush. *Police Systems and Practices*. Upper Saddle River, NJ: Prentice Hall, 1994.

Bouza, Anthony V. *The Police Mystique*. New York: Perseus Publishing, 2001.

Chamelin, N. *Criminal Law for Police Officers*, 7th ed. Upper Saddle River, NJ: Prentice Hall, 1999.

Collins, Pamela A., Truett A. Ricks, and C. W. VanMeter. *Principles of Security*, 4th ed. Cincinnati, OH: Anderson Publishing Co., 2000.

Goodman, D. J. *Enforcing Ethics*. Upper Saddle River, NJ: Prentice Hall, 1997.

Egger, Steven A. *The Killers Among Us*, 2d ed. Upper Saddle River, NJ: Prentice Hall, 2001.

Fyfe, James J., Jack R. Greene, and W. F. Walsh. *Police Administration*, 5th ed. New York: McGraw Hill, 1996.

Kappeler, Victor. *The Police & Society*, 2nd ed. Prospect Heights, IL: Waveland Press Inc., 1999.

Kerle, Kenneth E. *American Jails: Looking to the Future*. Boston: Butterworth-Heinemann, 1997.

Martin, Susan E. *Status of Women in Policing*. Washington, DC: Police Foundation, 1990.

Miller, L., and M. Braswell. *Human Relations & Police Work*, 4th ed. Prospect Heights, IL: Waveland Press Inc., 1996.

Oliver, Willard M. *Community Oriented Policing*, 2d ed. Upper Saddle River, NJ: Prentice Hall, 2000.

Peak, K. J. *Justice Administration*, 3rd ed. Upper Saddle River, NJ: Prentice Hall, 2000.

Peak, Kenneth J. *Policing America*, 3rd ed. Upper Saddle River, NJ: Prentice Hall, 2001.

Schmalleger, Frank. *Criminal Justice Today*, 6th ed. Upper Saddle River, NJ: Prentice Hall, 2000.

Seigel, L. *Criminology*, 7th ed. Belmont CA: Wadsworth, 2000.

Sheehan, R., and G. Cordner. *Introduction to Police Administration*, 4th ed. Cincinnati, OH: Anderson Publishing Co., 1999.

Shusta, Robert M., et al. *Multicultural Law Enforcement*, 2nd ed. Englewood Cliffs, NJ: Prentice Hall, 2001.

Stinchcomb, Jeanne B. *Corrections Today: 21st Century Challenges.* Upper Saddle River, NJ: Prentice Hall, 2002.

Terrill, Richard J. *World Criminal Justice Systems,* 5th ed. Cincinnati, OH: Anderson Publishing Co., 2002.

Weisheit, R. et al. *Crime & Policing in Rural & Small Town America,* 2nd ed. Prospect Heights, IL: Waveland Press Inc., 1999.

Weston, P., and K. Wells. *Criminal Investigation,* 8th ed. Upper Saddle River, NJ: Prentice Hall, 1999.

Williamson, Harold E. *The Corrections Profession.* Newbury Park, CA: SAGE Publications, 1990.

Wrobleski, H., and K. Hess. *Introduction to Law Enforcement & Criminal Justice,* 6th ed. St. Paul, MN: West Publishing Co., 2000.

About the Author

James D. Stinchcomb recently retired as the Director of the School of Justice and Safety Administration, the regional training center for all of Miami-Dade County, Florida. He was previously an associate professor in and chairman of the Department of Administration of Justice and Public Safety at Virginia Commonwealth University. He has served in Washington, D.C. as the criminal justice staff director for University Research Corporation and previous to that held a full-time consultant assignment with the U.S. Department of Justice under the Law Enforcement Assistance Administration's Law Enforcement Education Program (LEEP).

Previously the author served on the staff of the American Association of Community and Junior Colleges (AACJC) under a Kellogg Foundation grant as specialist for public services education. He was training and education staff supervisor for the International Association of Chiefs of Police under a Ford Foundation grant. He developed and chaired the Department of Police Administration at St. Petersburg (Florida) College and developed the bachelor's degree program in law enforcement offered at Florida State University. Both of these programs were first of their kind in the state of Florida.

After completing a Bachelor of Science degree in psychology, Director Stinchcomb served in the Louisville, Kentucky, Police Department. He holds a Master of Arts degree in criminology and completed all course work in the criminology doctoral program at Florida State University. During his years in Washington D.C., he was a lecturer in the Administration of Justice Program at the University of Pittsburgh and served as a part-time faculty member at eight other community colleges and universities.

In his consulting capacity, the author has visited more than 150 educational institutions to review and assess their efforts in law enforcement and criminal justice. He was the co-author of two AACJC publications: *Guidelines for Law Enforcement Education Programs in Community and Junior Colleges* and *Law Enforcement Training and the Community College.* In addition he was volume editor of the J. G. Ferguson Publishing Company's *Career Opportunities: Community Service and Related Specialists* and served for twenty years as series editor for all Prentice-Hall criminal justice publications, including both textbooks and training manuals.

During his career, Director Stinchcomb also served on staff and as consultant to the President's Crime Commission on Law Enforcement (his primary responsibilities included researching and writing the sections on police personnel, manpower utilization, education, training, and career development); the National Sheriffs' Association; the Westinghouse Justice Institute; the Public Administration Service; and a number of state and local organizations. He was an original member of the grant review panel for the Law Enforcement Education Program under the Law Enforcement

Assistance Administration (LEAA) and served as project director for the U.S. Office of Education grant to develop a curriculum guide for law enforcement degree programs. One major consultant role, for several years, was as criminal justice personnel specialist to the National Planning Association, Washington, D.C., in its study of manpower needs for criminal justice. He also serves regularly as an accreditation team member for the American Council on Education in its program to evaluate law enforcement training within the military. Director Stinchcomb is the author of several articles and chapters in college textbooks on police issues.

Most recently he has prepared education and training evaluation studies for police departments from Chicago to St. Petersburg, Florida, and New Orleans, Louisiana, and he has been called upon to testify regarding proper police training methods. He received the O. W. Wilson award from the American Criminal Justice Association in 1998.

Director Stinchcomb has an extensive background in managing grant-funded activities, some of which include developing a graduate program (LEAA), a Traffic Safety Center (VA), a Saudi Arabian Police Training program, Computer-Based Training Lab materials, a Juvenile Justice Use of Force curriculum, and a statewide study of the Test for Adult Basic Education for Criminal Justice Personnel. He also has assisted local and state governments in writing and preparing grant applications. Upon retirement, he became an associate in several firms that develop and provide police promotional examinations, and he serves as Executive Advisor to Kaplan College, a distance-education organization based in New York and in Boca Raton, Florida. Kaplan is providing distance education in criminal justice using a professionally based curriculum developed by Director Stinchcomb.